Earth, Sky, and Sculpture

THIS BOOK IS DEDICATED TO

THE MEMORY OF

RALPH E. ("TED") OGDEN,

1895–1974.

Earth, Sky, and Sculpture

STORM KING ART CENTER

ESSAYS BY

H. Peter Stern

Peter A. Bienstock

Irving Lavin

Joan Pachner

PHOTOGRAPHS BY

Jerry L. Thompson

STORM KING ART CENTER

Major funding for this book was provided by the Ralph E. Ogden Foundation, Inc., and Mr. and Mrs. James H. Ottaway, Jr., with additional support from Furthermore, the publication program of The J. M. Kaplan Fund.

PHOTOGRAPH CREDITS
All photographs by Jerry L. Thompson, courtesy the Storm King Art Center, except where noted otherwise. Page 56: fig. 3, Alinari-Scala/Art Resource; fig. 4, Alinari/Art Resource, NY; fig. 5, by permission of the British Library, 649.C.25 (1) Pl. 43. Page 58: fig. 6, Antony Miles, Ltd./Bridgeman Art Library; fig. 7, Tony Perrottet/Omni-Photo Communications, Inc.; fig. 8, Erich Lessing/Art Resource. Page 60: fig. 13, Stapleton Collection, The Bridgeman Art Library; fig. 14, The British Museum; fig. 15, Alinari/Art Resource, NY.

ISBN
Hardcover: 0-9606270-1-4
Softcover: 0-9606270-0-6

Printed and bound in Italy.

Contents

H. PETER STERN

The Creation of the Storm King Art Center: A Personal History

Where else can one enjoy roughly 125 of this century's best sculptures while walking around acres of rolling, beautifully landscaped lawns and wooded areas surrounded by distant, low-lying mountains? Storm King stands head and shoulders above other American sculpture parks—in size, the beauty of its grounds, the quality and range of its collection, and the care it takes in harmonizing art with the surroundings.

. . . Storm King's exceptional qualities are evident the moment one enters the grounds and catches sight of Alexander Calder's mammoth stabile The Arch *just inside the gate, Alexander Liberman's gigantic stridently hued* Iliad *a bit farther off, and Isamu Noguchi's regal* Momo Taro *crowning a low hill a few hundred yards away.*

One senses immediately that this is an enchanted world in which provocatively modern and critically approved sculptures representing today's largely urbanized culture can interact with surroundings that reflect nature-oriented and contemplative values and ideals.

THEODORE F. WOLF, *The Christian Science Monitor*, 1987

. . . there is no question that among sculpture parks of the world, Storm King is King.

J. CARTER BROWN

DIRECTOR EMERITUS

NATIONAL GALLERY OF ART, 1993

Storm King Art Center is the experiential sculpture museum. The visitor is freed from academic intermediaries to walk its five hundred acres and encounter sculpture one to one.

CANDIDA N. SMITH, *The Fields of David Smith*, 1999

If there is a heaven for sculpture we can be pretty sure of its exact location: 500 acres of rolling countryside nestled between Schunnemunk and Storm King mountains in the lower Hudson Valley, 60 miles north of New York City.

Unpretentiously, this aesthetic paradise is called the Storm King Art Center.

BENJAMIN FORGEY, *The Washington Post*, 2000

The Storm King Art Center is an unusual museum. Its collection is not constrained by the walls of the museum building. The floor of its main exhibition area is grass and fields. Walls are formed by trees and hills. The roof is sky. Placement of its large works is determined by the landscape. The space around the sculptures cannot easily accommodate other works. The selection process is guided not only by aesthetic or artistic considerations, but also by questions of durability, scale, and compatibility of the sculpture with the landscape. Storm King is not only a museum. It is a park as well, a beautiful landscape, critical in making it the "king of sculpture parks."

"You can find out how to do something and do it or do something and then find out what you did. I seem to be of the second disposition." So said Isamu Noguchi about his work. Much the same can be said about the Storm King Art Center. It was not planned, it was created. In 1960, none of the major sculptures that are the glory of Storm King yet existed. Sculptors were only beginning to make large-scale, abstract works. The property was one-third its present size. The planting of allées of trees and the massive creation of hills and wide, sculpted walking areas through fields of long grasses and wildflowers were not yet dreamed of.

Over the years, area by area, we sculpted the landscape. Into this landscape we "planted" sculptures, as if they were specimen trees, in spots where they would be seen to advantage from many angles and from near and far. Sculptures had to blend with the landscape; often the landscape was changed to fit the sculpture.

Two of the most common questions visitors to the Storm King Art Center ask are "How did it all start?" and "What was Ralph E. ("Ted") Ogden's and Peter Stern's vision?" It started with the land. Ted Ogden's and my responses to the beauty of our landscape and the drama of monumental sculpture challenged us over time to harmonize these two assets. We wanted to bring the interrelationship of a remarkable landscape and great sculpture to its full potential. We were not burdened by rigid ideas or concepts. Our museum has been a work in progress with every addition of a major sculpture, the planting of a tree, or the clearing of a vista presenting a different challenge and a new opportunity. We added a sculpture only if it interacted well with the landscape and the other sculptures.

It has been said that timing is everything. We opened our doors to the public in 1960, just when monumental outdoor sculpture began to appear and when large-scale sculptures were available at relatively low prices. Few museums or collectors had the space, or even the desire, to give each sculpture a generous setting.

Much of our success has come through our ability to see, and take advantage of, the opportunities we have had. The Ralph E. Ogden Foundation, Inc., acquired the property of a friend, Vermont Hatch, including a Normandy-style château, positioned on a plateau overlooking the valley between two mountains. Schunnemunk and Storm King Mountains form the "green walls" of what we came to recognize as our "outdoor galleries." The area around the building provided intimate exhibition space, whereas the surrounding fields, hills, and woods offered variety and space for larger sculptures. The removal of 2 million cubic yards of gravel from the property in the early 1950s, while the New York State Thruway was being built, created devastation. After the Art Center opened, we turned the depletion into an opportunity by putting equivalent yardage back in a creative manner. The château, now our museum building with its many windows overlooking the landscape, enabled visitors to see outdoor sculptures from additional vantage points. Its indoor galleries were too small for large-scale sculptures. In time this turned our attention more than ever to the outdoors.

We learned—and continue to learn—the art of siting and placing sculpture. A key participant in this process has been landscape architect William A. Rutherford, Sr. He had designed both Ted Ogden's and my gardens before the Art Center was established and has worked continuously with the Art Center from its beginning. With his help we were able to create a natural-looking landscape with perfect sites for future sculpture installations.

It is impossible to think of the Art Center without our gifted director, David R. Collens, who has been with us since 1974. In addition to his duties as director, he has also curated all of our outstanding annual exhibitions.

The Art Center has benefited from the support of the Ogden-Stern family. Ted Ogden, through the Ralph E. Ogden Foundation, Inc., bought the initial 180 acres, the Art Center's David Smith collection, and all works of art until his death in 1974. He also supervised landscaping projects. The depth of Ted Ogden's and my friendship went far beyond our family and business relationship. I have been chairman and president of Storm King from its beginning. After Ted Ogden's death, I assumed full responsibility for the purchase of major sculptures, for landscaping and policy decisions, as well as for administration. Major financial support for the Art Center continues to come from the Ralph E. Ogden Foundation, Inc., of which I am president; my three children, Lisa, Beatrice, and John, are trustees.

The creation of the Art Center would not have been possible without Star Expansion Company. Ted Ogden and I were joint owners until 1974, when I bought out his interest. In addition to capital contributions by Ted Ogden and myself in the early years, Star Expansion Company donated substantial funds in the 1970s and 1980s. These constitute the Art Center's Ogden/Stern Investment Fund. In 1997 Star was sold.

A museum of Hudson River painters was our first vision for use of the building. We held a major Winslow Homer exhibition in 1963 that included six paintings Homer completed during a long visit to Houghton Farm in Mountainville. But in 1961 the first sculpture had arrived, a work by the Austrian sculptor Josef Pillhofer. After much debate, Ted Ogden and

ABOVE
The museum building, designed by architect Maxwell Kimball and erected in 1935, was originally a private residence.

OPPOSITE
The Storm King Art Center affords visitors the opportunity to look from within the building to the surrounding landscape and to experience relationships between small sculptures or drawings and large, outdoor works. Here, during the third year of the three-year exhibition "The

Fields of David Smith," one could compare Smith's *Tower Eight* (Raymond D. Nasher, Dallas, Texas) indoors with *Tower I* (the Collection of Candida and Rebecca Smith) installed outdoors.

In an early use of open space as setting for sculpture, *Trinity* by Karl Pfann (1960) was placed south of the museum building.

With visible satisfaction Ralph E. ("Ted") Ogden rests his elbow familiarly on the "shoulder" of David Smith's *Personage of May*, one of thirteen Smith sculptures he had just purchased for the Art Center.

I placed it south of the building, drawing the eye to distant vistas and suggesting to the inner eye the vision of an exciting future of placing large sculptures. The dialogue between art and nature opened.

Much had to be done to make the former private estate more accessible to the public. We broadened roadways, created allées, built parking areas, and laid out lawns and walking paths around the building. Rooms inside the building were converted into galleries with proper lighting and wall space. We contoured the sharp and dangerous drop in elevation to the west of the building, which had been created during the building of the Thruway, and filled in the swamp in the valley below. When we cleared the woods to the north of second growth, vistas opened up. We borrowed many small sculptures and grouped them in the area where now only Alexander Calder's gigantic *Arch* stands. It was not until 1973, when Alexander Liberman's *Adonai* was installed, that our emphasis began to shift to monumental works.

Ted Ogden's great acquisition was a group of thirteen David Smith sculptures. He purchased them in 1967 from the sculptor's estate following a trip he made to Bolton Landing with his wife, Peggy, and daughter, Joan. The sculptures were placed close to the building. It was not until later that we grouped them together and displayed them with a view into the distance, much as Smith had done at Bolton Landing. We salvaged five gigantic stone columns from the Armstrong Mansion, Danskammer, on the Hudson River—demolished in 1932—and erected them as a salute to Thruway travelers. (Stones from Danskammer had been used in the construction of Vermont Hatch's weekend residence, now our museum building.)

Following Ted Ogden's death in 1974, most of the smaller loaned works were removed as I began to give priority to acquiring a permanent collection of large-scale sculptures. Kenneth Snelson's *Free Ride Home* was purchased in 1975. Isamu Noguchi's *Momo Taro* was installed in 1978. Mark di Suvero's *Mon Père, Mon Père* and *Mother Peace* were acquired in 1981, followed by Alexander Liberman's *Iliad* in 1981, Alexander Calder's *The Arch* in 1982, and Louise Nevelson's *City on the High Mountain* in 1984. Richard Serra accented the southern border of the Art Center with the installation in 1991 of *Schunnemunk Fork*. Four massive steel plates were partially sunk and integrated into a 10-acre site dedicated exclusively to this work. Magdalena Abakanowicz's *Sarcophagi in Glass Houses* was moved into a specially created site in 1994, the same year that Ursula von Rydingsvard's *For Paul* was purchased. In 1997 Andy Goldsworthy began his imaginative serpentine dry stone wall that curves among a line of trees in the southern part of the property. One year later, upon its completion, he titled it *Storm King Wall*. In 1998 Mark di Suvero completed *Pyramidian* as the centerpiece of our south fields.

Isamu Noguchi talks with John P. Stern at the Art Center's twenty-fifth anniversary celebration in 1985.

Landscape architect William Rutherford, Sr., and Andy Goldsworthy discuss the construction of *Storm King Wall* as Adrian Joyce looks on.

The creation of Isamu Noguchi's *Momo Taro* (1978) followed a two-year courtship of the living sculptor whose work in stone I most admired. Busy with other projects, Noguchi was reluctant to visit the Storm King Art Center. Once here, however, he succumbed to Storm King's opportunities and challenges. We instantly agreed on a location for his work, a hill overlooking the exhibition area and distant mountains. I resolved all questions with him in less than an hour. We enlarged and reshaped the hill according to his needs. I gave him unlimited time to finish the sculpture and freedom to change the design in any way he wanted. Noguchi responded to the trust and respect given to him by creating one of his greatest works. He became a friend and visited us many times.

In the early 1990s my wife, Dr. Margaret Johns, and I traveled to every site-specific sculpture Richard Serra had created before I invited him to make a proposal. In turn, Serra spent a year studying our landscape before he asked us for the exclusive use of a 10-acre farm field that seemed very far from the museum area. He spent another year coming up with the design for *Schunnemunk Fork*, a work inseparable from the land. Its understated angularity forms a frame, a contrast, a platform for the fields and hills.

Our newest site-specific installation is Andy Goldsworthy's 2,278-foot *Storm King Wall*. The beautiful dry stonework of the curving wall embraces trees, dives underwater, comes up again, and blends respectfully with the landscape. Originally we limited the length to 800 feet, but as the project progressed, we were overcome by its inner logic. We agreed to the extension of the wall to where it met the New York State Thruway and could go no farther.

This period of intensive acquisition of large-scale sculpture was matched by extensive landscape projects. The sharp drop-off to the valley on the east received a massive transfusion of gravel, turning it into a new outdoor gallery, one "tier" below the hilltop. It became the home for a number of Alexander Calder sculptures on long-term loan. A new allée of trees leads to a spacious site that was prepared for future visitor facilities near the middle of the property. We created hills and planted pine trees to hide approaching cars from view from the museum building area, while preserving exciting vistas to the south for approaching visitors. We extended the lawn area to the east of the building to create a new home for the outdoor David Smith collection so that it could be viewed with Storm King Mountain as a backdrop. We built dirt roads to the east and south to open up dramatic views for walkers and minibus tours. Areas in the northern and southern parts of the property have been prepared for future use as exhibition sites.

With the advice of experts at the Lady Bird Johnson Wildflower Center in Austin, Texas, including its landscape designer, Darrel Morrison, we have embarked on a new program to restore native long grasses and wildflowers on 80 acres of the property. A series of wide, contoured paths through the

Gigantic stone columns from the Danskammer mansion, erected at Storm King in 1964.

This reproduction of an Easter Island *moai* is a reminder of the universal and age-old tradition of monumental outdoor sculpture and was donated to the Storm King Art Center in 1972 by the Ralph E. Ogden Foundation, Inc. It was authorized by the Chilean government and purchased from the World Monuments Fund (of which H. Peter Stern was, and continues to be, Vice Chairman) to support their Easter Island restoration project.

long grass areas will provide access to sculptures. Another major undertaking is the planting of additional trees for beauty, shade, and definition.

Architect Joyce Rutherford worked with her husband, William A. Rutherford, Sr., and redesigned our buildings as our needs grew. We glassed in the former *porte cochère* (covered entrance) to the museum building and converted it into an information center and shop. We fitted offices and restrooms into the former kitchen, servant quarters, and garages, and converted the basement into a conference room. At the same time, we built two caretaker houses at the edges of the property to increase security. Two other houses on the property were remodeled and one moved out of view.

In 1977 the Storm King Art Center began to enlarge its Board of Trustees with the addition of J. Carter Brown (who still serves on the board) and Cynthia Hazen Polsky (who after twenty years of active service as vice chairman, continues as an honorary board member and chairman of the Acquisitions Committee). In 1978 we initiated a membership program. In 1987 the museum received accreditation from the American Association of Museums. With the help of The Horace W. Goldsmith Foundation, we began an education program, visitor services, and the training of a dedicated group of docents. Georgene Zlock, who in 1995 became full-time Administrator of the Art Center, has been my indispensable assistant on Art Center matters for more than twenty-eight years.

Peter A. Bienstock joined our board in 1985. He brought with him wide experience in land management. This was soon to become a major focus as we embarked on a program of viewshed protection with matching funds provided by the Dewitt Wallace Fund for the Hudson Highlands with the assistance of Barnabas McHenry. Thus we were largely able to preserve vistas as well as views into forests on landscape visible from the Art Center. Peter A. Bienstock's wide range of experience and wisdom in philanthropic and financial affairs led to his becoming our treasurer and chairman of the Executive Committee.

During the Art Center's first thirty years Star Expansion Company donated administrative, accounting, and groundskeeping personnel. Its engineers pioneered sculpture installation and conservation procedures that have been widely adopted by sculptors and conservators. In 1985 Star contributed 200 acres of adjoining land to the Art Center, doubling its size. In the same year it also donated 2,100 acres of Schunnemunk Mountain (now owned by Open Space Institute) to preserve the dramatic green backdrop for the sculptures.

The Art Center's major financial support continues to come from the Art Center's Ogden/Stern Investment Fund and the Ralph E. Ogden Foundation, Inc. The Art Center has attracted growing public support through its Friends program and has increased the number of its major

Alexander Liberman's
Adonai as it looked in 1997;
Alexander Calder's *The Arch*
stands in the background.

donors. We will continue to broaden the financial base for its unique operation.

In our ever more crowded world, the Storm King Art Center is a countermodel, a haven of spaciousness. Much of our task in the future will be to respect our achievement by maintaining and enhancing the uncluttered and generous use of space. Placement of new sculptures and special exhibitions must protect the long vistas for existing works. The Art Center needs to accommodate growth in popularity and attendance. At the same time it must retain its sense of tranquility and recognize the physical limitations of our delicate environment. We will preserve what has been created as we continue to dream and make plans for the future.

It is impossible to acknowledge the many ways in which so many people have helped the Storm King Art Center. At the very least, I would like to list the members of our loyal and able Board of Trustees and our Officers. In doing so, I must say a special word of thanks to the most senior member of the board, Leslie A. Jacobson. For thirty years his wise advice on legal and policy matters to Storm King and the Ralph E. Ogden Foundation, Inc., has been invaluable.

PETER A. BIENSTOCK

Art in Nature: Storm King and the Sculpture Garden Tradition

Then the Lord God formed man of the dust of the ground, and breathed into his nostrils the breath of life; and man became a living soul. And the Lord God planted a garden eastward, in Eden; and there He put the man whom He had formed. And out of the ground made the Lord God to grow every tree that is pleasant to the sight, and good for food; the tree of life also in the midst of the garden, and the tree of knowledge of good and evil.

—GENESIS 2.7-9

PRECEDING TWO PAGES
Richard Serra's *Schunnemunk Fork* in its first season during the summer solstice of 1992. Newly planted long grass has covered all signs of excavation and installation. Already the sculpture cooperates serenely with the landscape, becoming part of its 10-acre site.

OPPOSITE
Although they are clearly girder and I-beam constructions, Mark di Suvero's *Mother Peace* and *Beppe* inhabit the landscape like giant beings that may be about to walk away.

FOLLOWING PAGES
Pages 46–47
The original installation on the Calder hillside in 1988: as one ascended the incline, Calder's sculptures gradually came into view; *Cheval Rouge*, *Tom's*, *Five Swords*, *The Red Feather*, and *Le chien en trois couleurs*.

Page 48
Looking toward the west "wall" of the Art Center— Schunnemunk Mountain— the eye is drawn to David von Schlegell's untitled open squares floating improbably over the field in the middle distance.

Page 49
Looking toward the east "wall" of the Art Center—the Hudson Highlands.

Pages 50–51
In the gorge of Moodna Creek.

From the earliest writings of recorded civilization, the concept of the garden appears: nature at its most beautiful, benign, and bountiful. But always nature contains the danger of chaos and destruction, and the balance must be maintained by humankind's skill, labor, and sound judgment.

Whether it be Eden, or the peace the Buddha experienced under the bodhi tree, or the paradisiacal garden of Islam, the idealized image of nature as a place of bliss, inspiration, and sanctuary is integral to civilization. And so people have continually sought to create gardens containing the most beautiful of nature's plants, trees, and flowers, enhanced by still and flowing waters, and protected against wild animals, storm, and fire.

From at least ancient Greek and Roman times in the West, statuary and sculpture have been included in gardens. Often they bring the wild back into tamed nature, in forms that do not threaten, as with sculptures of beasts and hunters, or of the hoofed Pan with his irresistible pipes. More often, images of beautiful men and women complement the beauty of the place, or those of wise men suggest and highlight the profundity of one's experience of the garden itself.

The garden historian William Howard Adams has noted:

> *Within each part of the landscape of Greece—the mountains, hills, islands, seascape—there existed a genius loci, and it was the builder's duty to identify this sacred spirit peculiar to each location. Only after the spirit was divined could the architecture itself be introduced into a holy partnership with the existing features of the topography. As man-made environments, gardens as well as architecture must ultimately find a way into the natural world, the ordinary landscape.*

(*Nature Perfected: Gardens Through History,* Abbeville Press, 1991, p. 29)

The Storm King Art Center continues this rich and venerable tradition of the garden as expressing the *genius loci* and presents it in a form that incorporates the aesthetic vision of the twentieth and twenty-first centuries. What may not be immediately evident to the visitor to Storm King (as it would equally not be immediately evident to the visitor to Frederick Law Olmstead and Calvert Vaux's Central or Prospect Parks) is that he or she is in a great garden, whose lands have been almost totally altered by the hands and minds of artists. Vast amounts of soil have been moved; hills and valleys created; vegetation removed and replaced by carefully selected trees, shrubs, and flowers; and new vistas and viewpoints opened by the shifting and carving of earth and rock.

At Storm King, the garden has been planned to receive specific, exceptional monumental works of sculpture; the architecture of the landscape is at the service of, and in partnership with, the artists themselves. Thus an area of perhaps 10 acres is devoted entirely to the four great steel plates of Richard Serra's *Schunnemunk Fork.* The area chosen is a sloping field, the rise of which enhances the impact of the work, with the great palisade of

Schunnemunk Mountain up and beyond. The field is kept in grasses to maximize the power of the work and the sweep of the eye across it and to the mountain.

The grand scale of Storm King is utilized to enrich the viewer's appreciation of the works on display. Mark di Suvero's great girder constructions can be viewed from a quarter mile away, like magnificent Jurassic figures marching across the landscape; then one can move under them and experience their power at close range.

Storm King, like Tivoli or Versailles, allows visitors to alternate between the intimate and the public. One can amble in the peace of the woods and be suddenly surprised by lovely and fascinating works of modest size or one can walk across an open hilltop filled with large and colorful Calder stabiles.

All the while during a visit to Storm King, one is aware of the garden and of nature beyond the garden. The heart of the Art Center's grounds is the fine Normandy-style stone museum building, and radiating out from it are fields and hills containing major works of sculpture, with a number of works visible from almost any point. But also visible are the forested hills of the Hudson Highlands to the east and of Schunnemunk Mountain to the west. As one moves from the core area of the Art Center to the north, south, and east, woodlands take over—with the dramatic gorge of Moodna Creek to the east—and the frequency with which one encounters sculptures lessens.

The sense of the ordered and peaceful garden, surrounded by nature left to its own devices, enhances the sense of sanctuary afforded by Storm King. The Art Center is furnished by people, both with plants and with art, while the area around it is governed by nature's imperatives rather than by those of human beings. Yet the distant and wilder landscape is also magnificent and compelling. Much of the crafted plantings and sculpted landforms of Storm King are abstractions from and echoes of that natural vista.

Storm King, then, presents two kinds of experience, one intellectual and spiritual and the other primitive and natural. Its carefully shaped landscape and superbly chosen and sited art are in the great tradition of the sculpture garden: its margins, blending into the wild and finally merging into it, suggest the elements of nature that have captivated humans but that have also challenged them, and which they have for thousands of years sought to bring under their control and into their service. Few sculpture gardens in the world so dramatically unite these elements, and no other garden of modern sculpture can be said to have made so ambitious and successful an effort to do so.

The uniqueness of Storm King consists in the fact that, although it contains great sculpture, perhaps the greatest sculpture of all is the brilliantly crafted landscape itself, set in the splendid panorama of the natural landscape.

IRVING LAVIN,
Institute for Advanced Study, Princeton, New Jersey

Storm King:
The Genius of the
Place

Figure 1
The Storm King Art Center
with Mark di Suvero's
Pyramidian, looking east past
the New York State Thruway
to Storm King Mountain.

Figure 2
View west from the Art
Center, past di Suvero's
Mother Peace and the New
York State Thruway toward
Schunnemunk Mountain.

Figure 3
Tribolo, *Hercules and Antaeus,* fountain, ca. 1540. Florence, Villa Medicea di Castello.

Figure 4
Bernardo Buontalenti, *Prima Grotta,* 1583–1588. Florence, Giardino di Bòboli.

Figure 5
The Pagoda in the Royal Gardens at Kew. From William Chambers, *Plans, Elevations, Sections, and Perspective Views of the Gardens and Buildings at Kew in Surrey,* London, 1763.

Storm King is an extraordinary, indeed, unique experience. Approaching this Sanctuary—which is how I tend to think of it—eastward from the busy New York State Thruway, surrounded by the ancient looming humps of the Appalachian Mountains, one cannot elude the feeling that one is entering an enchanted world (fig.1). In the middle distance Mark di Suvero's huge *Pyramidian* (pyramid + meridian), melding earth and heaven in its very name, announces the principal theme of the place. Although it may be said to have resulted from the convergence of many factors, personal as well as circumstantial, and to incorporate many historical ingredients, artistic as well as ecological, the Storm King Art Center, in the valley between Schunnemunk and Storm King peaks, is ultimately without precedent, and even—despite its renown and widespread influence—without real parallel.

In a profound sense the placement of sculpture—that is, nonfunctional, human-made objects—in the landscape is inevitably, if unconsciously, a reflection of our conception of our own relationship with the world around us. The modern history of that conception begins in the Renaissance, when people rediscovered and sought to emulate the fabled villas and gardens of antiquity. Often this emulation consisted simply in reinstalling fragments of ancient statuary in outdoor settings. But often also both objects and nature were manipulated to create large-scale, complex works of art, ultimately quite different from their ancient prototypes, in which the relationship is explicitly defined. Essentially three approaches emerged. In the formal garden the ideal order discernible in the natural world was extrapolated and distilled into visible perfection, with humankind exerting its superior intelligence and will upon the wild forces of confusion and profusion. At the Villa Medicea di Castello near Florence, the fountain of Hercules and Antaeus is a metaphor for the ruling dynasty of the city: the wrestling figures are raised high above the polygonal basin and surrounding parterre; just so, in the sculpture itself, the ancient hero defeats the bestial adversary by lifting him above his mother earth, the source of his otherwise invincible power (fig. 3). At the opposite extreme was the equally artificial realm of the grotesque, in which the confusion and profusion of the natural world were themselves augmented into a patently unnatural display of subterranean amorphism. In the famous grotto of the Giardino di Bòboli earthly creatures are literally part of the landscape, as were Michelangelo's unfinished Slaves (later moved to the Galleria dell'Accademia and replaced by plaster casts) (fig. 4). Here our human rationality glimpses the primordial chaos of its alter ego. Finally, there is what might be called the "natural" nature familiar to us from the English park. Viewed from a "picturesque" distance, sheep and deer and hoary hermits (sometimes paid actors) appear withdrawn from sophisticated society, ruminating the real meaning of it all. It is no accident that the characteristic human-made feature of the English park was not a sculpture but an often ruinous or fragile architectural "folly," a term that gives ironic but pure expression to the essential artifice and ephemerality of human endeavor (fig. 5). I do not think it a gross exaggeration to say that the modern history of articulating the relationship between humankind and landscape consists in permutations of these alternative but complementary conceptions.

What then is it about Storm King (I hesitate to call it a landscape or a park) and these artworks (I hesitate to call them simply sculptures) that makes such powerful magic? Of course, magic is by definition uncanny, but I suspect that at least in some measure the explanation lies in the innovative character of the institution itself and the work it has achieved. I would classify these distinctions as physical (scale), aesthetic (relationship between objects and setting), intellectual (program and meaning), and social (relationship between patron and audience). There are partial precedents in all these respects, but not, I believe, for what Storm King represents as a whole, the *genius loci.*

Large-scale sculpture obviously has an ancient history. If one thinks of the megaliths ("big stones") of Stonehenge and the gigantic stones heads of Easter Island (figs. 6, 7), one might well identify the emergence of civilization itself with the urge to augment not only the quality of human creativity—sophisticated tools, farming and husbandry, community living—but also the scale. On the other hand, size alone is an insufficient measure of the significance of these "superhuman" monuments. The unimaginable ingenuity and labor involved in carving and erecting such works would be meaningless without an understanding of the context in which they were meant to be seen, if only because the stones were transported long distances to their carefully chosen sites, on the Salisbury Plain, or on great artificial island platforms literally "facing" inland. They define the landscape and seem to embody in themselves the awesome vastness of the world they inhabit. Or think of Egypt, one of the earth's most ancient civilizations, where super-life-size human figures were created virtually from the outset (fig. 8). We call such works colossal, a concept invented by the Greeks—to whose mentality it was originally quite foreign—precisely to comprehend those outlandish Egyptian giants (Herodotos uses the word *colossal* exclusively for that purpose); the Greek sense of scale being determined by reference to the human body, colossal is ultimately an anthropomorphic notion. The alternate term *monumental* derives from the Latin word for "reminder" and has inherently nothing to do with size; its use in reference to size imputes anthropomorphic measure to the value of recollection. Neither of these concepts is applicable at Storm King, where the sense of scale is conveyed by the relationship between the objects and the environment, which includes the sky as well as the land. Earth and sky are physically conjoined by Alexander Calder's vaulting figure called *The Arch*, which seems to spring from the earth to reach for the sky and complete its arc (fig. 9). Mark di Suvero's *Mother Peace* actually includes the landscape in the transparent sign language of its message, which is to say Peace on (Mother) Earth (figs. 10, 11). Storm King thinks big, and the visitor to this other-world is lifted up and out of our ordinary, anthropomorphic existence to become something akin

ABOVE

Figure 6
Stonehenge, 1800–1500 B.C.
Salisbury Plain, Wiltshire.

Figure 7
Stone Heads, on the slope
of Ranu Raraku, 17th century
or earlier. Easter Island.

Figure 8
Colossi of Memnon
(Amenophis III, ca. 1390–ca.
1353 B.C.).

OPPOSITE

Figure 9
Alexander Calder, *The Arch.*

Figure 10
Mark di Suvero, *Mother
Peace.*

Figure 11
Mark di Suvero, *Mother
Peace*, detail.

Figure 12
David Smith, *Three Ovals
Soar.*

Figure 13
Maerten van
Heemskerck,
Colossus of Rhodes,
engraving, 1572.

Figure 14
Pietro da Cortona,
*Deinokrates Shows
Mount Athos to
Pope Alexander VII*
(1655–1667),
drawing. London,
British Museum.

Figure 15
Giambologna, *The Appenine*,
ca. 1583. Pratolino, Villa
Medici.

to those ancient nature spirits—what else are David Smith's *Three Ovals Soar* (fig. 12)?—of which, or of whom, we human beings have been subtly aware ever since we became conscious inhabitants of this world. Landscape-embracing sculptures were conceived in antiquity: the Colossus of Rhodes stood astride the harbor of that city (fig. 13); Deinokrates offered to carve Mount Athos into a figure of Alexander the Great holding a city in his hand (fig. 14). The idea was reiterated by Giambologna in his mountainous (containing a chamber in the head) personification of the Appenines in the garden at Pratolino (fig. 15). But nowhere else has a portion of the land and sky the size of Storm King been appropriated exclusively to the display of artworks conceived on a correspondingly mythic scale.

Measurements quite apart, many of the objects at Storm King were conceived in relation to a specific site, which was also frequently reconfigured to suit its new inhabitant. I am aware of no precedent for this degree and magnitude of conflation between nature and art. The sculpture and its setting seem to have been, and in large measure actually were, made for each other. Isamu Noguchi went to Japan, selected the stones, and shaped them together with the underlying hillock to create his *Momo Taro*, named for a mythical boy-hero born from a peachstone, whose conquests made him practically synonymous with the territorial and national destiny of Japan (fig. 16). One cannot properly speak of Storm King as a garden or even as a park since nature as such is not here an end in itself. Nor can we properly speak of an outdoor museum, since nature is not just the setting but an active participant in the show. David von Schlegell's significantly untitled aluminum squares—mysterious, glistening, fragile quadrupeds from some outer space of the mind—alight and give suspenseful life to the meadow around us (fig. 17). The powerful surge of Robert Grosvenor's untitled steel arc raises the very curvature of the earth to the explosive tension of a bow spring (fig. 18). At every turn the view is populated by things human-made to suit, while the character of the landscape—its nature, one might say— is defined by the objects it contains. The relationship is profoundly reciprocal. This is the reason I use the terms *landscape* and *sculpture*, which define separate domains, only reluctantly, *faute de mieux*: at Storm King the two categories fuse in a new kind of vision for which, in truth, we have no ready name. Symptomatic of this fusion is that traditional pedestals rarely intervene between the two domains.

Storm King does not recount the kinds of "stories" we associate with traditionally programmed garden sculptures that glorified important patrons, as in the great villas of the Renaissance, or celebrated civic heroes in public parks. Nor, on the other hand, are the sculptures purely "ornamental," or even pleasure giving in the usual sense—no waterworks, no fountains! Storm King is not Tivoli, or Versailles, or Central Park. Indeed, there is a certain austerity about the place. And all this mainly for two reasons.

Figure 16
Isamu Noguchi, *Momo Taro.*

Figure 17
David von Schlegell,
untitled.

Figure 18
Robert Grosvenor, untitled.

61

Figure 19
Alexander Liberman, *Iliad.*

Figure 20
Richard Serra, *Schunnemunk Fork* (with Schunnemunk Mountain in the distance).

Whatever their particular "subjects," the objects at Storm King were acquired and situated as works of art, with a view (pun intended) primarily to their visual qualities and relationships to one another and to their settings. Moreover, the works are for the most part abstract in nature (pun intended) and hence convey different kinds of meaning in ways different from those of traditional outdoor sculpture. At Storm King this meaning often lies precisely in the relationship between art and nature, the one conditioning the other. Alexander Liberman's *Iliad* stalks across the earth like the armored Achilles before the walls of Troy, resounding with the hollow clangor of bloody war (fig. 19). The four tines that constitute Richard Serra's *Schunnemunk Fork* measure and are measured by the surrounding space and the underlying terrain, which they penetrate as if to impregnate the great mountain in the distance whose name they also bear and with which they are thus literally merged in a single act of creation (fig. 20). (Poseidon plunged his trident into the Acropolis to engender the spring that made Athens possible.) The landscape acquires meaning from these sculptures, and vice versa. To the degree that they are abstract, the works at Storm King may be described as "pure" sculpture without anecdotal, representational, or narrative intent (although certainly not without content). By the same token the landscape is conceived as pure form, and not because it is artificially constrained into regular patterns, as in a French formal garden, or because it is artfully disguised as rustic nature perceived in a picturesque "view," as in the English park. At Storm King the settings, even distant mountains, co-respond in equal partnership with the works of "sculpture" on display. How can one ever again study the spatial intersections of gracefully branching limbs without thinking of David Smith's *Study in Arcs* (fig. 21)? And vice versa. Or see George Rickey's *Two Planes Vertical-Horizontal II,* without

gasping at the wonder of trees growing straight up on an inclined plane
(fig. 22)? And vice versa.

Finally, as an independent, privately sponsored foundation, Storm King
is not an appendage of some other entity, be it a noble residence, a branch
of government, a business enterprise. And Storm King was conceived from
the beginning as a public facility. In this sense it represents a new dimension of social consciousness and responsibility in the appreciation of nature
as well as art.

The mythic scale, the ideal intermarriage between humanity and
nature, the reach for universal expression and meaning, and the reciprocity
between private citizen and society at large—in all these innovative aspects
Storm King reflects its creation in a specific place and time, the United
States after World War II. In this sense Storm King is also a uniquely American experience. Nothing conveys the fundamental, sometimes seemingly
incongruous, values embodied in this experience more movingly than the
magnificent, also uniquely American prospect westward from the upper ter-
race toward the mountain horizon (fig. 2, page 55). The picturesque vision
includes that equally magnificent creation of the American dream, the New
York State Thruway, with its equally magnificent human-made objects of
our daily lives, reincarnated Conestoga wagons, lumbering bravely across
our field of comprehension into an unknown but promising future. It's the
American way. And it's a magical place.

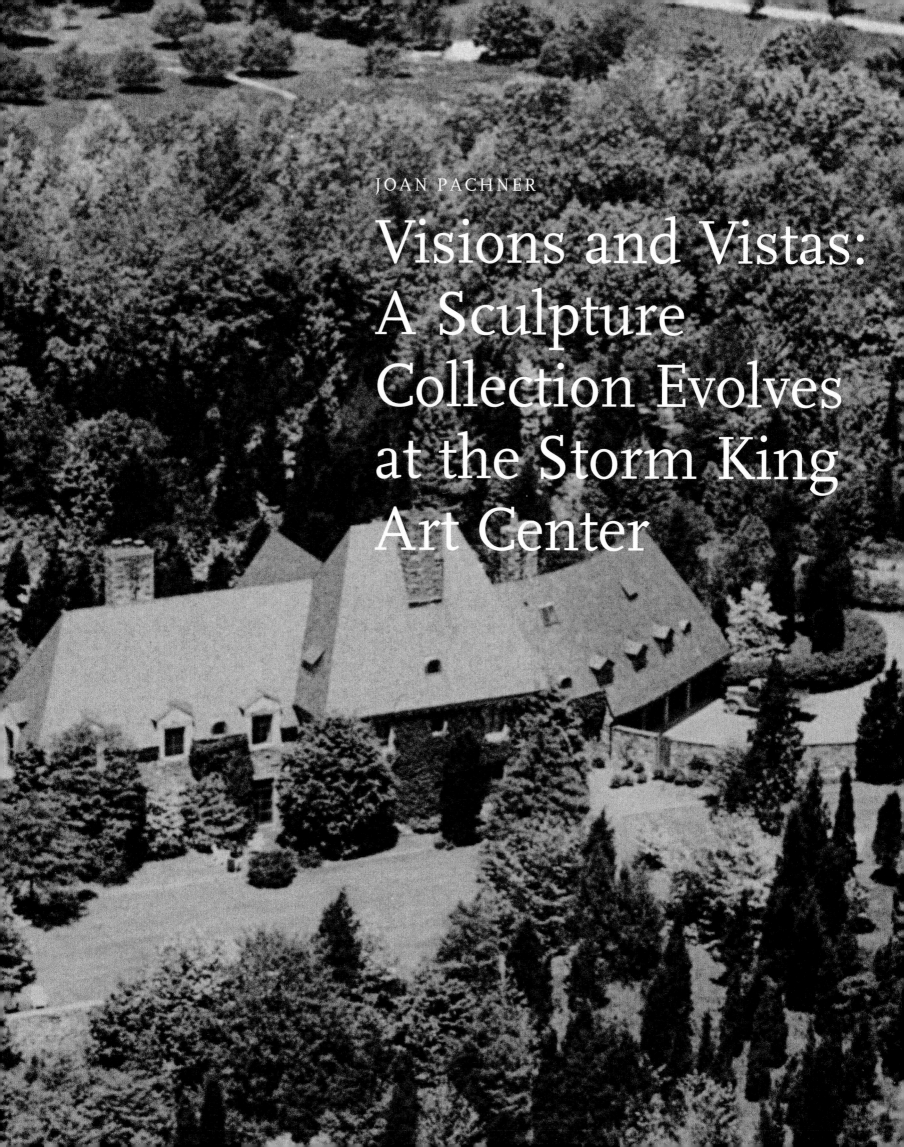

JOAN PACHNER

Visions and Vistas: A Sculpture Collection Evolves at the Storm King Art Center

PAGES 64–65
The Vermont Hatch Estate
in May 1946, later to
become the Storm King Art
Center. Photograph by
Sheriden and Maney.

THIS PAGE
Works acquired in the early
1960s for the new Art
Center. Clockwise from top
left: Joseph Pillhofer's
Man in the Quarry,
Fritz Wotruba's *Walking
Man,* Emilio Greco's
Large Bather I, and Alfred
Hrdlicka's *Golgotha.*

The sculpture collection of the Storm King Art Center has a personal quality. It has largely been shaped by the vision of two men: Ralph E. Ogden (1895–1974), who founded the Art Center in 1960 and guided its development until his death in 1974, and H. Peter Stern, who has served as the Art Center's chairman and president since its inception. The sculptures at Storm King must be viewed in light of the specially created landscape setting in which they are displayed and with a sense of the personal connection between the unique institution and its artists.

In 1959 the Ralph E. Ogden Foundation, Inc., purchased a weekend retreat from the estate of Ogden and Stern's friend Vermont Hatch, and in 1960 the Storm King Art Center was created. The initial purchase included a 30-acre property with a Normandy-style château and a formal flower garden. There were no views out from this area, as the property was overgrown. The land dropped off precipitously at various places, necessitating the immediate installation of fences for safety. The Art Center was then one-third its present size, and the property's natural beauty had been significantly scarred in the 1950s by the removal of more than 2 million cubic yards of gravel for construction of the new New York State Thruway.

The Ogden Years

Between 1960 and 1974 Ralph E. ("Ted") Ogden's vision determined the Art Center's development. Ogden, who was trained as a civil engineer, had retired from his position as chairman of Star Expansion Company. He particularly enjoyed working with the land—farming as well as road building. Though Storm King was conceived as a museum devoted to artists who painted in the Hudson Valley, as early as 1961 Ogden acquired his first sculpture. Yet it took almost a decade before the Art Center began to redefine its mission as a museum devoted to the display of large-scale sculptures in a natural setting of sweeping vistas.

In 1961 Ogden traveled to a stone quarry in Vienna near the Hungarian border. There he bought a large carved stone sculpture by the Austrian artist Josef Pillhofer (*Man in the Quarry* [1960]), the first of many such purchases destined for display in the Art Center's eighteenth-century-style formal gardens. In the early 1960s, Ogden acquired the cubic bronze *Walking Man* (1952) by the Viennese master Fritz Wotruba, the expressive carving *Golgotha* (1963) by Wotruba's protégé Alfred Hrdlicka, and the stately *Large Bather I* (1956) by the Italian Emilio Greco. Wotruba was recognized for his squared, sober, limestone carvings, and in 1959, because of his influence, Vienna was for the first time since the seventeenth century called "one of the capitals of sculpture" in the world. These works represent the continuation of a vital figural tradition.

Sculptures by European artists still constitute an important aspect of the Storm King collection. While American collections commonly display the work of American artists, there are few venues in this country where one can see examples of sculpture created in post–World War II Europe.

The principal catalyst for a definitive change in the Art Center's direction came in 1967 when Ogden visited the home and studio of the recently deceased David Smith at Bolton Landing, a village on the shore of Lake George in upstate New York. There he saw rows and rows of Smith's large metal sculptures set in the fields, ringed by the Adirondack Mountains. The Ralph E. Ogden Foundation, Inc., soon purchased thirteen works from Smith's estate and donated them to the Art Center. The sculptures, created in the last decade of the artist's life, include excellent examples of his varied working methods—from cast-bronze welded assemblages (*The Sitting Printer* [1954–55], *Personage of May* [1957], and *Portrait of a Lady Painter* [1954/1956–57]), to burnished steel works (*XI Books III Apples* [1959] and *Three Ovals Soar* [1960]), to the painted steel *Study in Arcs* (1957), *Tanktotem VII* (1960), and *Five Units Equal* (1956). *Volton XX* (1963) exemplifies Smith's later return to direct welded assemblages incorporating found objects. The Storm King collection includes examples from Smith's well-known Tanktotem and Voltri-Bolton series, as well as lesser-known sculptures that represent seminal aspects of his oeuvre.

At first, the thirteen Smith sculptures were placed in various locations surrounding the museum building. Following the David Smith retrospective of 1976, five sculptures, because of their smaller size and more delicate surfaces, were moved indoors to a special gallery. The eight sculptures exhibited outdoors were then grouped together for the first time along the southern edge of the hilltop, with an unobstructed view of the Hudson Highlands in the distance. The visual interaction of the sculptures with one another and with their surroundings recalled the effect of their original display in Smith's Bolton Landing fields. Over the next ten years the Art Center expanded; other sculptures were sited nearby, and the edge of the hill no longer formed the outer exhibition boundary. As a result, in 1988, the area behind the building was subtly reshaped and extended, and the Smith works on display were reinstalled as a group with a view to the profile of Storm King Mountain behind them. This focused exhibition area affirms the importance of Smith's sculptures to the Art Center and to the history of art.

[Text continues on page 84.]

ABOVE
A detail of the shovel/head
of David Smith's *Personage
of May*.

OPPOSITE
Portrait of a Lady Painter as
installed for the exhibition
"The Fields of David Smith."

ABOVE
The "palette" of David
Smith's *Portrait of a Lady
Painter,* a cast element that
appears in another Smith
sculpture as a head.

ABOVE
A detail of the burnished
stainless-steel surface of
David Smith's *XI Books III
Apples*.

OPPOSITE
XI Books III Apples in 1988.

74

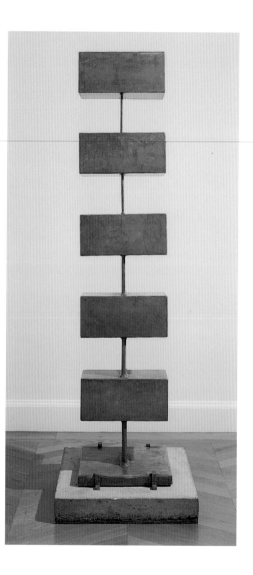

David Smith sculptures with delicate surfaces are kept indoors. Left to right: *Tanktotem VII,* *The Iron Woman, Five Units Equal, Raven V, Albany I.*

As the Art Center developed its approach to the display of sculpture outdoors, Ogden's collecting efforts intensified. He had purchased two sculptures by Barbara Hepworth: *Forms in Movement (Pavan)* (1956; cast 1967) and *Square Forms with Circles* (1963) in 1968 and 1969, respectively. The former is a fluid, gestural composition, exemplifying a lyrical strain in Hepworth's work that emerged in the 1950s. Its title refers to a somber, stately court dance of the sixteenth century. This work contrasts with the tall, planar bronze abstraction *Square Forms with Circles,* which reveals Hepworth's renewed interest in regularized, large-scale compositions.

In 1967 the Art Center purchased *Six Lines in a T* (created 1965–66/79), its first kinetic sculpture by George Rickey. *Two Planes Vertical-Horizontal II* (1970) followed in 1971 and *Five Open Squares Gyratory Gyratory* (1981) in 1992. *Six Lines in a T*—a classic Rickey—is an elegantly simple arrangement of rocking lines that move unpredictably in the breeze. It marks an important break with the artist's earlier sculpture and exemplifies the mature later work that he began to produce when he was fifty-eight years old. While *Six Lines in a T* was not designed for its present location, the glade in which it is now sited was chosen to expose it to gentle winds but not to the overwhelming gusts that prevail in an open expanse.

Both Rickey and Smith used burnished stainless steel for brilliant effect. Although Smith began burnishing in 1956 and Rickey in 1961, Rickey was apparently unaware of Smith's innovations. The two artists' mediums are similar, yet their works are very different. Rickey's sculptures since the 1960s have been resolutely non-objective, while Smith's compositions almost always retain a connection with the natural world. The two artists were friends. Smith taught Rickey how to weld when they crossed paths in 1954 at the University of Indiana, Bloomington (where Smith made *The Sitting Printer* [1954–55]). It is appropriate that their works stand together in perpetuity at Storm King.

Shortly after the Hepworth sculptures entered the collection, Ogden sought to acquire an important work by the master Henry Moore, a mission he entrusted to H. Peter Stern. Ogden had seen photographs of Moore's sculptures in the pastoral landscape surrounding his home and studio in Much Hadham, England, and felt that Moore's vision was compatible with his own. Stern went to visit Moore and decided to purchase the cast-bronze *Reclining Connected Forms* (1969), though at the time it was only a drawing. The sculpture is a horizontal, abstract restatement of the nested images that Moore began in the early 1930s and continued as an extended Mother and Child series. This contained image necessitated a more defined setting than did Storm King's larger sculptures; today it can be viewed in a carefully designed glade bordered by trees.

[Text continues on page 92.]

Two works by Barbara
Hepworth: above, *Forms in
Movement (Pavan)*; right,
Square Forms with Circles.

OPPOSITE
George Rickey's *Two Planes
Vertical-Horizontal II*.

ABOVE
Rickey's *Five Open Squares
Gyratory Gyratory* and
Six Lines in a T.

PAGES 88–89
Henry Moore's *Reclining
Figure II* (on loan from the
Museum of Modern Art,
New York) and *Reclining
Connected Forms*.

ABOVE
Henry Moore's *Reclining Connected Forms.*

OPPOSITE
Moore's *Reclining Figure II* (on loan from the Museum of Modern Art, New York).

Sol LeWitt's *Five Modular Units.*

While Storm King was acquiring works by established artists, it also supported those at an earlier stage in their careers. In 1971 the Art Center purchased *Five Modular Units* (conceived 1966; fabricated 1971), one of Sol Lewitt's first outdoor steel Minimalist sculptures. His predictable, direct, and visually comprehensible work represented a systematic rejection of qualities associated with European art, as well as with Abstract Expressionist art (including that created by David Smith, characterized by an improvisational working method, organic form, deliberate irregularity, and a rough human-made finish). The purified effect of LeWitt's regular form is enhanced by its placement in a rural setting where the geometric scaffold contrasts with the irregularity of nature, as well as with other sculptures in its visual field.

"Ted Ogden liked size and he liked scale," according to Stern. The accuracy of this recollection is born out by the projects that Ogden nurtured during the years he devoted to the Art Center. Ogden's own preferences intersected with those of artists who sought to create works on such a scale that they could not be accommodated by traditional museum or residential structures. The Art Center presented wonderful opportunities, for it was a museum where the floor was grass and the ceiling was unbounded; there were no walls or other architectural constraints.

Around 1970 the Art Center began to earmark specific areas on the property as sites where artists could develop large unique projects of a kind they could never develop elsewhere. In 1972 David von Schlegell created the Art Center's first site-specific sculpture: three large, open, stainless-steel squares supported by legs to form open cubes set in an undulating field. While the tripartite work is architectural in scale, its impact is discreet and its reflective material contributes paradoxically to the work's delicate presence. The geometric forms also serve as a metaphor for the presence of humans in the landscape, an effect that the artist himself related to Chinese paintings in which architectural structures are dwarfed by vast landscapes. The legs of the cubes are of varying lengths because each touches the ground at a different elevation. Seen from the hillside, the squares appear to hover, but from the top of the the hill they seem to rest on the ground. One can also walk through the cubes and experience the squares as framing elements of an ever-changing *plein-air* painting. (Von Schlegell had studied with his father, a well-known American Impressionist painter.) The sculpture then directs our gaze away from the ground, out to the distance and up to the sky; it intensifies our connection to nature.

ABOVE
David von Schlegell's untitled three-part, site-specific work in morning mist. Originally the only sculpture in the view south from the entry drive, von Schlegell's work is now joined by Mark di Suvero's *Pyramidian* and Siah Armajani's *Gazebo for Two Anarchists: Gabriella Antolini and Alberto Antolini.*

OPPOSITE
Another untitled work by David von Schlegell surprises walkers in a wooded area; its shiny surface collects and heightens the soft light filtering through the trees.

Tal Streeter's *Endless Column* with Alexander Calder's *The Arch* in the distance. The red and black of the two works respond to the orange-over-green coloring of fall in a complex manner, unlike their simpler contrast to the deep greens of summer.

The Art Center was uniquely able to develop sites for large sculptures that could not be accommodated elsewhere. Tal Streeter's dramatic 70-foot-high *Endless Column* (1968) was initially installed in Central Park at the corner of Fifth Avenue and Seventy-ninth Street in July 1970, as part of the "Sculpture and the Environment" exhibition in New York City. Two years later the tall, red-painted sculpture came as a loan to Storm King Art Center, where it was placed in a large, open field. It was purchased in 1977. The movement of a sculpture from an urban setting to the Art Center's rural surroundings soon became a familiar trajectory. For instance, Alice Aycock's *Three-Fold Manifestation II* (1987), acquired ten years after the Streeter, had also been installed in New York City (at the entrance to Central Park at Fifth Avenue and Fifty-ninth Street) prior to its arrival at Storm King. Streeter's *Endless Column*, named in homage to Constantin Brancusi's *Endless Column* in Tirgu Jiu, Romania (1937; cast iron, 8' 1/2" high), was conceived as a "ladder into the sky," a means to draw the gaze upward, against gravity.

Certain of Ogden's acquisitions provided early lessons about potential difficulties that the Art Center would encounter when large sculptures were permanently installed outdoors, subject to wind, rain, snow, and other dangers unknown to traditional museums. On one occasion a zigzag portion of Streeter's *Endless Column* was sheared off during a windstorm. The tall structure was also repeatedly struck by lightning, blackening and blistering its brightly painted surface. This problem was ultimately solved, by Lester O. Knaack, an engineer and vice-president at Star Expansion Company, who suggested that an internal lightning rod be installed.

Robert Grosvenor, inspired by the relation of Storm King's gently rolling field to the distant mountain range, proposed a dynamic, 200-foot-long, 12-inch-wide, black arc, a painted steel composition with a flat central panel. It was conceived in 1970 and fabricated in 1974. Installation of the weighty, long, thin sculpture, however, presented logistical challenges and required specialized heavy machinery, including a hydraulic lift. Knaack suggested anchoring the sculpture to underground concrete bases, an ingenious solution that would apply to the installation of future large-scale works as well.

This expansive, horizontal structure bridges the field and creates an immediate correspondence with the view to the Hudson Highlands, a link completely appropriate for the Art Center both then and now. Of equal importance, the sculptures by von Schlegell and Grosvenor reveal the romantic side of artists initially thought to be exponents of cool geometry. Both men used industrial materials associated with the modern world as a means to open viewers to the surrounding natural beauty. The potential for industrial materials and nature to enhance one another has been observed since the mid-nineteenth century; it is a potential realized dramatically at the Storm King Art Center. The two experimental works are now classics in the Storm King collection.

OPPOSITE
The towerlike structure of Alice Aycock's *Three-Fold Manifestation II* seems to invite one to climb its series of "landings"—an impossible endeavor. As nonfunctional architecture it somewhat resembles a garden folly.

PAGES 100–101
Robert Grosvenor's untitled steel arc makes a totally different gesture by hugging the ground and rhyming with the distant mountain.

The refabrication of *Adonai*
progresses in early 2000. A
scale model indicates the
arrangement of the cylindrical forms.

Adonai (1970–71), a large assemblage of rusted oil drums (29' 6" x 63' x 52' 8") by Alexander Liberman, was one of the last major sculptures that Ogden brought to the Art Center. Its installation in late 1972 presented technical challenges that Ogden relished solving, with assistance from Knaack and landscape architect William A. Rutherford, Sr. The sculpture, however, was made of inherently perishable materials—oil drums that had already been underground for twenty years when the artist bought them in bulk at public auction in 1970. *Adonai* was originally constructed on a level gravel lot outside the artist's studio, but when it was installed in the uneven field at Storm King, its central horizontal element was pitched at an angle, putting the entire structure under stress. Protective coatings were not applied to the tanks for many years, causing them to corrode further; numerous welds broke, and the sculpture became structurally unsound. To save this superb example of Liberman's early monumental sculpture, it was refabricated in 2000, a solution the artist fully supported.

Ralph E. Ogden died in the fall of 1974. The Art Center, which had been in operation for almost fifteen years, was on its way to an increasingly clear self-definition, but it was still in transition. A few large sculptures had been acquired, but a hundred small sculptures (the majority on loan) were scattered in the lower fields. Moreover, the property as a whole was undeveloped; a master plan had not yet been conceived.

During its refabrication,
Alexander Liberman's
Adonai dwarfs the surrounding industrial equipment.
Suggesting a giant in
captivity, the sculpture
clearly belongs in the out-of-
doors.

The refabricated *Adonai* in the summer of 2000, newly installed in the sculpture's original location. With time and additional attention, the work's surfaces will acquire a more even patina of rust, and its platform of exposed earth will fill with grass.

Alexander Liberman's *Iliad*, acquired by the Art Center in 1981.

Two views of Alexander Liberman's heroic *Adam;* one with the landscape as backdrop and another more private glimpse. An opening in the trees was specially designed to accommodate the view of the figure from behind.

The Stern Years

Following Ralph E. Ogden's death, H. Peter Stern assumed full responsibility for the Art Center. At the same time, many artists were creating large sculptures that could not be displayed in traditional gallery or museum spaces, or even in the homes of most collectors. The Storm King Art Center was an exception—a museum that sought to display large-scale work and had the space to accommodate it.

Stern refined the Art Center's mission; it would now emphasize the equal importance of sculpture and landscape, separately and together. Sculptures are exhibited with ample surrounding space, visible from many directions and from long distances. The dramatic sight lines incorporating great steel sculptures, trees, lawns, and fields in a natural arena of distant mountain ranges cannot be matched by other institutions. The large sculptures together in the vast landscape—including, for instance, Alexander Calder's *The Arch* (1975) at the museum entrance, Alice Aycock's *Three-Fold Manifestation II* (1987) atop the north hill, and Mark di Suvero's works in the south fields—-create their own visual rhythm and cadence, complementing the density of the trees and the lyricism of the rolling fields.

The first large-scale sculpture that Stern acquired for the Storm King Art Center was Kenneth Snelson's majestic *Free Ride Home* (1974; aluminum and stainless steel; 30 x 60 x 60'). Stern was immediately struck by the work when he saw it installed in the spring of 1975 on a barren, concrete 2-acre plaza in back of the newly developed Waterside Plaza apartment towers in Manhattan. He envisioned it transported to the Art Center's rural environment, set amid the grass and trees. Within a few months *Free Ride Home* was installed on a specially landscaped grassy area, designed by William A. Rutherford, Sr. Snelson's architecturally scaled, open, latticework sculpture appears as light as a constellation of stars. The self-supporting structure depends on a push-pull system invented by the artist in the winter of 1948–49, in which wire cables function like muscles and the metal tubes like bones, suspended in an internally generated taut balance of tension and compression. Buckminster Fuller (Snelson's teacher at Black Mountain College in North Carolina) coined the word *tensegrity* to describe the system. The nature-based structural mechanics are the essential subject of Snelson's work.
Free Ride Home represents a moment of physical expansion in his oeuvre. The soaring form began as a maquette of metal tubes and knotted strings (Columbus Museum of Art) arranged around a central core and extended in three directions with three arches. One of the arches reminded Snelson of a bucking horse, so he named the work after a racehorse, Free Ride Home. The mathematical basis of this sculpture was determined at a small scale. When the artist came to erect the sculpture, he laid the components on the ground, fastened the wire to the tubes, and enlisted four local men for two hours to hoist it into the air. The structure has never required any adjustment.

Delicately poised on only three points, Kenneth Snelson's *Free Ride Home* creates a soaring, graceful arc made entirely of straight lines.

Art Center director David R. Collens with Mark di Suvero during the installation of the 1985 Mark di Suvero exhibition.

Art Center chairman and president H. Peter Stern with Mark di Suvero at the installation of *Pyramidian* in 1996.

Mark di Suvero's career has been closely entwined with the Art Center's evolution. The juxtaposition of a broad expanse of nature with his bold, open steel structures embodies the goal of the Storm King Art Center to create a unique environment in which the dynamism of art and nature reinforce each other. Mark di Suvero began his career in the late 1950s and came to public prominence in the mid-1970s with a display of his work in the Tuileries Gardens in Paris (1974) and a major retrospective the following year at the Whitney Museum of American Art in New York, which also included the installation of his large sculptures in public sites through all five boroughs of the city. But where would the huge sculptures go after the exhibition was over? Di Suvero accepted an offer from H. Peter Stern to place his sculptures outdoors at the Storm King Art Center and asked to place them in an open field to the south of the hill where the museum building stands. At that time the site seemed far from the "top of the hill"; it was accessible only to those willing to climb down and up a steep incline.

In 1976 Mark di Suvero installed five massive sculptures in the field in a giant arc formation, using industrial cranes, cherry pickers, welding equipment, and a crew of assistants. The group included *Are Years What? (For Marianne Moore)* (1967), *Oneoklock* (1968–69), *Mother Peace* (1969–70), *Ik Ook* (1971), and *Mon Père, Mon Père* (1973–75). When the area was recontoured to eliminate a clifflike drop, di Suvero moved his works farther into the distance and arranged them in a more spacious configuration.

The Art Center presented two major exhibitions of di Suvero's work, the first in 1985 and the second in 1995–96, and currently owns an unrivaled group of four of his major sculptures, including *Mother Peace, Mon Père, Mon Père, Mozart's Birthday* (1989), and *Pyramidian* (1987/98). Di Suvero's works reveal his ability to use industrial elements in monumental, architecturally scaled, spatially dynamic compositions that convey poignant human emotion.

Mother Peace, a three-dimensional peace symbol, was the last major work that he completed before leaving the United States for voluntary exile in Europe (1971–75) in a personal protest against America's involvement in the Vietnam War. While di Suvero was abroad, his father died; the evocative *Mon Père, Mon Père* was created in homage. *Mozart's Birthday* exemplifies a different formal development. The sawhorse configuration contains various elements, including flat circular shapes of various sizes and numerous acute angles created by the I beams.

The largest di Suvero work in the Storm King Art Center collection is the 65-foot-high *Pyramidian*, a commanding openwork composition. The suspended interior beam directs our gaze in various directions; it is large without being overbearing. Taller than the surrounding trees, *Pyramidian* visually anchors the large southern end of the property.

[Text continues on page 129.]

Mark di Suvero with his welding torch, at work completing *Pyramidian* in 1998.

A view of the Mark
di Suvero installation at
Storm King in the winter
of 1976–1977. Photograph
by George Bellamy (pre-
ferred photo credit of
Richard Bellamy [1927–
1998], di Suvero's longtime
friend and representative,
whose photographs consti-
tute an important di Suvero
archive).

FOLLOWING PAGES
Works by Mark di Suvero.
Pages 118–119, looking
southeast at *Mon Père,
Mon Père* surrounded by
blossoming crab apple, dog-
wood, and rhododendron.
Alexander Calder's *Five
Swords* can be seen in the
background; pages 120–121,
two views of *Mother Peace*
in the height of summer;
pages 122–123, *Mother
Peace* and *Pyramidian* on a
misty late summer morning;
pages 124–125, *Mon Père,
Mon Père* in early spring and
winter.

Two views of Mark
di Suvero's *Pyramidian*.

While the collection of large-scale sculpture burgeoned at Storm King, other less monumental projects were also nurtured, including Patricia Johanson's site-specific *Nostoc II* (1975), nestled in the woods. As the first commissioned work created entirely on-site with materials exclusively from the property, *Nostoc II* is also an important piece in the evolution of the Storm King Art Center. This, the first work in the collection by a contemporary woman artist, is composed of boulders and large rocks set on the ground in a 350-foot area punctuated by tall trees. Its overall form is based on the molecular structure of a chain of blue-green algae. Johanson's work rejects the single focus of traditional sculpture. Instead of presenting an object to be looked at and walked around, she creates space to be walked through and discovered; an overall scheme emerges only through physical interaction with the sculpture. The artist brings people to nature through art and to art through nature.

In 1975 the Art Center decided to concentrate its display on the permanent collection and supplement it only occasionally with loans. After having cleared the fields of a multitude of smaller sculptures, Stern, together with the Art Center's new director, David R. Collens, began to acquire large sculptures appropriate for the unique environment that was being created at Storm King. By the next season only a small group of carefully chosen works was on view, including Alexander Liberman's *Adam* (1970) and *Adonai* (1970–71), as well as Tal Streeter's *Endless Column* (1968) and the site-specific works by David von Schlegell and Robert Grosvenor.

Patricia Johanson's *Nostoc II* was the first sculpture at Storm King to be made of natural materials from the Art Center property. Later, work by Andy Goldsworthy would show an affinity with Johanson's deliberate blurring of the distinction between sculpture and landscape.

Members of Isamu Noguchi's crew cooperate on the tricky installation of Noguchi's *Momo Taro*.

Noguchi with Mihoko Masuda, daughter of his assistant, inside the "peach half" of *Momo Taro*.

OPPOSITE
Momo Taro as seen from the bottom of the hill "behind" the work, though, like many works of modern sculpture, this one eludes such ideas as "front" and "back."

The Art Center set on a course to expand its collection in a very selective manner, choosing only artists and works of art with the clear potential to develop a relationship with the landscape. Isamu Noguchi, admired for his unparalleled ability to blend aesthetic achievement with function, was invited to build a stone sculpture that incorporated seating. Noguchi visited the Art Center in 1977, surveyed the landscape, and selected a site. Within a year, he created a nine-piece, 40-ton granite sculpture titled *Momo Taro* (1977–78) to rest atop a specially landscaped hill with commanding views of the surrounding area; it is considered to be one of his masterpieces. The specially constructed, dramatic setting on a high mound is a reminder of Noguchi's long involvement with theater design; the mound itself was created at the artist's request by Art Center landscape architect Rutherford.

Noguchi created *Momo Taro* at his studio on the Japanese island of Shikoku. With the Art Center's topography in mind, he consulted many site photographs and measurements gathered during his visit. His assistant searched for granite boulders on the nearby island of Shodoshima and found one too large to move; it had to be split. The act of splitting the rock reminded Noguchi and his assistants of the story of Momo Taro, a Japanese folk hero who was said to have emerged from the split halves of a peach pit. The roughly carved-out center of one of the stones evokes the split pit, while the smoother outer surface suggests the skin of a peach.

Momo Taro by its nature encourages visitors to sit on its benches and to climb into its rounded form. Noguchi hoped that visitors—especially children—not only would climb into the cavity but also would sing inside the "peach pit" and enjoy its special aural resonance. *Momo Taro* is one of three works in the Storm King collection that can be sat on, climbed in, and touched. (The other two are Siah Armajani's *Gazebo for Two Anarchists: Gabriella Antolini and Alberto Antolini* [1992] and Daniel Buren's *Sit down* [1998].) While Noguchi is well-known for creating fully orchestrated environments, on this occasion he set his carved stones into surroundings whose ultimate evolution would be out of his control. Yet the cultivated environs continue to support the harmony of Noguchi's carefully wrought and arranged stones.

Most sculptures at the Storm King Art Center have been conceived independently of the Art Center's topography. Works are sited with the intention of melding a sculpture with its new location, a collaborative process—involving Stern, Collens, and landscape architect Rutherford—that often entails physically reconfiguring the land. Works by Alexander Calder, Louise Nevelson, Siah Armajani, Ursula von Rydingsvard, and Magdalena Abakanowicz were all installed in this manner.

[Text continues on page 138.]

PRECEDING PAGES
Pages 132–133, *Momo Taro* in full sun.

ABOVE AND OPPOSITE
Details of Noguchi's sculpture showing the varieties of texture in the granite.

134

Momo Taro in soft, gray winter light.

Momo Taro in early spring.

Momo Taro on a clear summer day with thick foliage and deep shadows. The sculpture is especially sensitive to changing light; its coloring alters subtly, sometimes dramatically, and its forms trade places in prominence, depending on whether they are in light or shadow.

On a soft, overcast day in fall. The smaller of the two cavities in *Momo Taro* is visible only in a raking light; it disappears completely in full sun.

Following the Noguchi commission, Stern pursued a monumental stabile by Alexander Calder and in 1982 purchased *The Arch* (1975), one of the artist's last projects. Its siting at the Art Center's entrance was determined after much discussion. The black painted stabile is one of the first works visitors see when they drive through the Art Center gate. The ground on which the sculpture stands was subtly raised 4 feet, a solution devised by Rutherford that enables visitors to see the work fully from a distance. The open parabolic arch entices visitors to pass through its portal and discover the joys of the buoyant forms that Calder endowed with the energy of nature.

The Calder purchase proved so successful that the Art Center pursued a group of the artist's stabiles as long-term loans to enhance the artist's presence. In 1988 a new sculpture platform was inaugurated behind the museum building, linking the upper hill to a lower field. The area was enlivened with Calder stabiles and since that time has been known as the Calder Hillside. The original group, which included *Five Swords* (1970), *Chien Tricolore* (1973), and *Cheval Rouge* and *Tom's* (both 1974), as well as *The Red Feather* (1975), has changed over the years.

The bright red *Five Swords* derives its name from the curved elements that recall the shape of a scimitar; it is a beacon to visitors as they walk around the southern end of the property. *Black Flag* (1974) came to the Art Center during the 1999 season. At times its abstract shape recalls an oversized insect or bird whose scale has transformed its "legs" or "wings" into arches. The title describes the formal triangular flag projecting atop the sculpture. While the flat surfaces are painted flat black, they appear as a symphony of grays, for each plane reflects the light at a different angle.

Calder began creating architecturally scaled stabiles in the late 1950s and early 1960s. As he became absorbed with the engineering and structural challenges posed by the large works, he gradually retired from making the smaller mobiles that had defined his early production. Often working from small models, Calder created full-scale stabiles such as *Five Swords* and *Four Planes Escarpé* in collaboration with the factory workers in Biémont, France; *The Arch* was fabricated at Segre Iron Works in Roxbury, Connecticut. He was intimately involved in all construction details, including the cutting of the steel shapes and the bolting and painting of each work. The painted stabiles looks surprisingly light and buoyant, defying the weight of the material. The organic forms of Calder's later stabiles are firmly rooted in his personal history of created forms and themes. Works such as *Chien Tricolore* recall his career-long engagement with animal themes, including *The Circus*. Every step we take in, under, and around these sculptures changes our view of the surroundings and provides both a sense of shelter and a new measure of our own scale. The works of Calder, exhibited outdoors "where the sky could be my ceiling," are a vitally important part of Storm King's collection.

[Text continues on page 152.]

ABOVE AND OPPOSITE
Two radically different views of Alexander Calder's *Black Flag*, courtesy Calder Foundation, New York, from the east and the south. For all its complexity, the sculpture retains hints of a familiar biomorphic form. It seems to stride across the lawn with conscious intention.

FOLLOWING PAGES

PAGES 140–141
The Calder hillside at Storm King in 1988 (left to right): *Cheval Rouge, Tom's, Le chien en trois couleurs, Five Swords, The Red Feather.*

PAGES 142–145
Three views and a detail of *The Arch.*

ABOVE
Detail of *Le chien en trois couleurs.*

OPPOSITE
Le chien en trois couleurs as it was reinstalled in 1999, near the edge of the woods.

Five Swords in winter; in the background are Richard Serra's *Schunnemunk Fork*, the maple allée, Mark di Suvero's *Pyramidian*, and Schunnemunk Mountain.

FOLLOWING PAGES
The Calder hillside as it appeared in 1997 (left to right): *Cheval Rouge, Five Swords, Four Planes Escarpé, Le chien en trois couleurs.*

In 1984 Louise Nevelson's fabricated painted steel assemblage *City on the High Mountain* (1983) rounded out the Art Center's collection of works by modern masters. Nevelson, beginning in the 1940s, made her reputation with boxed constructions of found and discarded wood. Many of her installations were theatrically presented, the effects amplified by controlled lighting. Nevelson herself was a dramatic presence and had spent much of her lifetime engaged with the worlds of theater and dance. In the mid-1960s she began to use fabricators to create works out of steel. Nevelson turned away from her characteristic medium, but her method of foraging for material remained unchanged. Working with a crew of assistants, she became her own artistic director.

In 1983 Nevelson, scavenging her own work, decided to combine elements of models of two separate projects that lay dormant at the Lippincott foundry, located at that time in North Haven, Connecticut. These models had been made seven years earlier, when official commissions for her monumentally scaled, fabricated work proliferated. They reflected an increased openness in her compositions, away from the rigid box-forms that had defined her production since the mid-1950s. The leftmost section of *City on the High Mountain* (which stands on its own base) was initially part of the curvilinear ribbonlike Louise Nevelson Plaza on William Street in downtown New York City (1977). The rightmost section was reused from the rectilinear *Model for Sky Tree* (1976), a design created for the Embarcadero Center in San Francisco. Nevelson connected the two sections with sweeping curvilinear elements and various found objects, creating a new composition that fully subsumed its parts. Within the year she had her 10-foot-high model enlarged to its full height of about 20 feet. She selected additional elements from a special scrap pile collected for her by Lippincott and added them to create the final composition. These included the "lace" (a found element from the factory floor commonly recycled in her work at this time; it reminded her of lace doilies from her childhood) and the rectangular "gong." The ball of railroad spikes that crowns the work, probably crafted in the early 1970s, was placed last. Nevelson explained, "Sometimes it's only a period that really finishes the sentence and that was the period that finished that sentence." The dense, lively composition brings the artist's urban sensibility to Storm King's rural setting. The characteristically black, complex assemblage is one of Nevelson's larger creations; it is among the very best of her late steel sculptures.

Installing permanent sculpture outdoors presents challenges not faced by traditional museums. Sculptures are anchored to the ground, usually with an underground support; they cannot be easily relocated. Therefore, in order to determine the optimum placement of *City on the High Mountain*, the Art Center built a full-scale wooden model, which could be moved with relative ease. The experience of looking carefully at the work in various

ABOVE
Louise Nevelson talks with H. Peter Stern on the occasion of the Storm King Art Center's twenty-fifth anniversary in 1985; the artist strolls with her assistant, Diana MacKown, at the rainy opening of the Nevelson exhibition in 1983.

OPPOSITE
Louise Nevelson's *City on the High Mountain* as seen from the museum building.

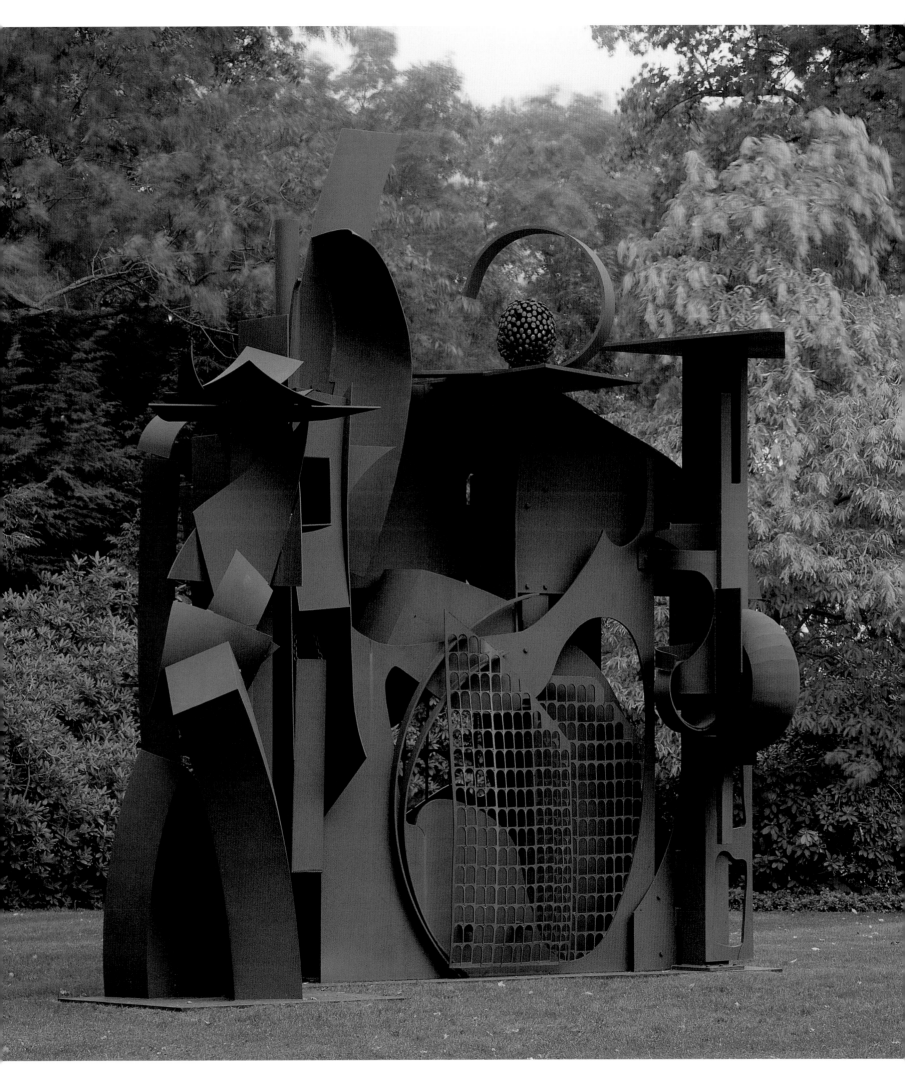

OPPOSITE
Louise Nevelson's *City on the High Mountain*.

RIGHT
Details of Nevelson's *City*, showing the variety of its many "neighborhoods."

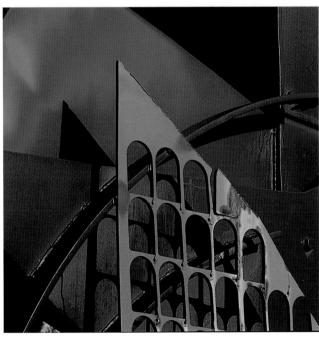

surroundings led to its siting in an area that is very different from the spacious one surrounding Calder's *The Arch*. *City on the High Mountain* is a stagelike work, one with a clearly defined front and back. Its layered composition recalls a grouping of stage flats. The sculpture was therefore installed in its own proscenium space near the museum building, where it is framed from most vantage points by a backdrop of densely planted trees. This solution also allows visitors to see the work from inside the museum building.

Unlike *City on a High Mountain*, Ursula von Rydingsvard's massive wood construction *For Paul* (1990–92) demanded a spacious setting. From a distance, the graphite-coated work looms large. But a close-up view rewards visitors with rich details including saw marks and chinks that give the structure its special character. In 1992, for the artist's first solo museum exhibition, Collens and the artist placed the 14-foot-high sculpture on the edge of the lawn, near a tall oak. In the fall of 2000 the work was relocated to a lower elevation on a specially designed hillside. The new site allows viewers to look down into the sculpture's hollow inner chambers, revealing an important dimension previously visible only from the second floor of the museum building. This process of siting and resiting sculptures illustrates the degree to which the Storm King Art Center values the symbiotic relationship between sculpture placement and landscape design.

For Paul, which was built over a two-and-a-half-year period, is constructed from 4- by 4-inch western red cedar beams. The majestic structure evolved from a low, honeycomb piece that had been exhibited in 1990 and returned to von Rydingsvard's studio, where she transformed it into a tall, structure built around twelve bowls seamlessly melded to one another. The shape of the work's exterior protuberances was defined by its interior hollows. After a number of cedar beams had been stacked and cut, they were glued to one another and connected internally with dowels. Then, wielding a circular saw, von Rydingsvard hacked the outer surface, embedding her roughly drawn imprint into the milled wood. The surface was finished with powdered graphite, a technique she pioneered in the late 1970s. The scarred surface evokes the wear and tear of nature that one might associate with Henry Moore's sculptures, but her large-scale work creates its own landscape and contains many autobiographical references. Gray wood surrounded von Rydingsvard during the childhood years she spent in German relocation camps following the end of World War II. The process of tearing at the wood recalls her father's work as a forester, as it also evokes the tensions that existed between father and daughter. The work is a psychological landscape as well as a commanding physical object.

Von Rydingsvard's 1992 exhibition featured two additional outdoor works, including the site-specific *Land Rollers* positioned on the edge of the hilltop. It was composed of seventeen tarred and scarred cylindrical elements (fashioned in von Rydingsvard's characteristic manner from

ABOVE
Magdalena Abakanowicz in
Lyon, France, at work on
Sarcophagi in Glass Houses.

OPPOSITE
One element of *Sarcophagi
in Glass Houses* with
Schunnemunk Mountain in
the background.

4- by 4-inch cedar beams) with smooth ends, laid side by side on the ground. The low-lying sculpture drew visitors like a magnet as it appeared to mysteriously extend directly into the allée of maple trees in the distance below. The sculpture transformed the discontinuous physical space around it into a continuous pictorial image, eliminating one's view of the middle distance, and creating a fiction that joined near and far, above and below. *Land Rollers* was a spectacular accomplishment achieved with a minimum of means, a true marriage of an object with its site, where it remained for two years.

Von Rydingsvard created *Ene Due Rabe* with the Storm King Art Center's landscape in mind, although it was first exhibited in San Francisco, at the Capp Street Project gallery. At ground level, the thigh-high wooden structure—with its gridlike plan and gouged wooden oval craters—looked as if it could be an oversized game board. The work's title repeats words that Polish children often repeat before beginning a game, something like "one-two-three." It was intentionally installed on the lawn where it could also be clearly viewed from the second floor of the museum building. The aerial vantage point enabled visitors to see the sculpture fully, its own craggy landscape contrasting with the Art Center's lawns and fields.

Magdalena Abakanowicz's *Sarcophagi in Glass Houses* (1989) also has roots in history, while at the same time it resonates with contemporary life. Abakanowicz stripped nineteenth-century wooden turbine molds of their decorative and technical trimmings and discovered an analogous relationship between the rounded form of the engine and the human belly, each a container of heat and energy. The prone forms became "sarcophagi," which the artist set on separate platforms and enclosed in iron-frame glass houses. The iron-frame houses, fabricated in Abakanowicz's native Poland, both protect the interior elements and conceptually contain the implied energy they generate. The houses spark many associations; they can be greenhouses, stimulating the growth of the organic forms within, or prisons or cages, containing and separating the enclosed forms from the outside world.

The sarcophagi of Abakanowicz's *Sarcophagi in Glass Houses* are separated from one another and from the viewer, who cannot touch the sensuously carved forms inside. The poignant composition recapitulates themes of violence, decay, and loss explored by the artist throughout her career, yet it simultaneously expresses a sense of healing, as it contains the metaphoric seeds of hope, of rebirth. Its genesis lies in the artist's wrenching experiences during World War II as an adolescent in Poland and her life under a subsequently repressive Communist regime. The ground-hugging sculpture is installed on a spacious tract of land (400' long x 100' wide) raised subtly above an open field, its visibility augmented by a forested background. The architecturally scaled work remains mysterious and poetic, defying a single explanation; its multivalent character draws visitors repeatedly to its site.

Magdalena Abakanowicz's *Sarcophagi in Glass Houses* with the Hudson Highlands visible through a scrim of spring trees in early leaf. The dry winter wheat in the foreground is at the end of its life cycle.

Magdalena Abakanowicz's *Sarcophagi in Glass Houses* in winter, with stubble of tall grass in the foreground. The starkness of the season is in keeping with the ominousness that is one of the aspects of the artist's work.

Some sculptures, like *City on the High Mountain*, are to be looked at, while others are designed for full physical interaction. One of these is Siah Armajani's *Gazebo for Two Anarchists: Gabriella Antolini and Alberto Antolini* (1992). The Iranian-born Armajani, who lives in Minneapolis, is renowned for his politically resonant, large-scale, interactive environmental works that merge sculpture with architecture. The Storm King structure of two gazebos joined by a central bridge may represent the enduring bond of the brother and sister anarchists, tested by separation when the "dynamite girl" was convicted of transporting explosives in 1918. A bridge is often seen as a metaphor for communication of ideas, as well as for physical transportation, but this narrow bridge suggests frustration, not connection. Rutherford designed a simulated stream of plants and rocks to flow under the sculpture's "bridge" in order to underscore the metaphor of this central element. But the constricted interior space of Armajani's sculpture subverts the relaxing experience one anticipates from a gazebo. Once inside, one discovers that views of the expansive scenery are often blocked by thick diagonal struts. This physical constriction creates a sense of psychic unease. The sculpture interacts with the world around it, but rather than reinforcing our expectations, it subverts them.

Siah Armajani's *Gazebo for Two Anarchists: Gabriella Antolini and Alberto Antolini.*

Two views of Armajani's
Gazebo for Two Anarchists;
the work as it spans a
simulated "stream" and the
interior with its disturbing
evocations of incarceration
and execution.

Richard Serra in 1991 in the
meadow as one of the steel
plates of his *Schunnemunk
Fork* is lifted from its trailer.

The Art Center's mission to create a unique place for the integrated display of sculpture in nature has been especially fulfilled in the past decade by the addition to the collection of major site-specific commissioned works by Richard Serra and Andy Goldsworthy.

Richard Serra's *Schunnemunk Fork* (1990–91) was constructed on a 10-acre farm field that, at the time, was the southern edge of the Art Center property. Serra surveyed the Art Center grounds and chose the large, rolling field with its natural border of nearby woods, a site that had never before been considered for its artistic potential. He arrived at his final composition through a complex process that involved consulting both topographical maps and a surveyor, as well as walking the grounds with his wife, Clara Weyergraf-Serra. The work consists of four weathering steel plates set lengthwise and inserted into the ground at designated intervals. Each plate is 8 feet high (just taller than the viewer; arresting without being overpowering) and 2½ inches thick; lengths vary from 35 feet to almost 55 feet. Roughly a third of the length of each rectangular plate is visible; the remainder is buried in the earth. The visible angles correspond to 8-foot drops in the terrain. The title refers to the four-pronged, splayed schema; it also underscores the relationship between the site and nearby Schunnemunk Mountain.

The self-effacing work acts as a topographical marker, drawing one's attention to the land itself, more than to its industrial elements. Each plate functions as its own horizon and as a regular measuring device amplifying changes in the land underfoot. With deceptively simple means, Serra brought a previously unnoticed area of the property into sharp focus. While the sculpture can be viewed through the lens of a high-powered telescope sited near the museum building, it can best be enjoyed by visitors who walk to it, navigate the spatial divisions created by the steel plates, and take in the sculpture's visual connection with Schunnemunk Mountain in the distance. When Serra's work was first installed, it seemed to be very far from the museum building, which still remained the Art Center's primary focus. With the passage of time, newly developed walking paths and additional sculptures were installed in adjoining areas, drawing increasing numbers of visitors to the area pioneered by Serra.

While *Schunnemunk Fork* has not changed, the sculpture's site has undergone a series of subtle modifications that reflect broader landscaping developments at the Storm King Art Center. At first, the grass around the plates lay untouched; it grew wild and high right up to the steel. The high grass, however, discouraged visitors from entering the spaces created by the sculpture, so mowed paths were created. Hay bales harvested by a local farmer periodically punctuate the landscape, linking the property's agrarian past with the present. New plantings of native grasses and wildflowers will further vary this evolving landscape.

[Text continues on page 179.]

ABOVE
Serra and one of his riggers guide a plate as it is lowered into place.

RIGHT
Serra leveling one of the plates.

OPPOSITE
One of the giant steel plates of *Schunnemunk Fork* emerges from the snow.

FOLLOWING PAGES
Richard Serra's *Schunnemunk Fork* is complemented by objects with utterly different form and feeling—round bales of newly harvested hay.

BELOW

The weathering steel surface of one of the plates of Richard Serra's *Schunnemunk Fork* alters with time.

OPPOSITE

A plate rises above the tall grasses of early summer. During the work's first season at the Art Center, the edges of the steel rusted into a burning orange.

In 1995 the British artist Andy Goldsworthy was invited to consider a site on which to make a sculpture. He walked the grounds on numerous occasions and was drawn to the remains of a fallen-down farm wall in a wooded area about a half mile south of the Art Center's museum building. The dilapidated wall spoke of the land's agrarian past. It also reminded Goldsworthy of a meandering stone wall sculpture (1991) he had made in another former farmland, at Grizedale Forest in Cumbria, England. While walking through this area on the Storm King property, Goldsworthy discovered a row of trees that had grown along the wall's linear path. Although the trees' alignment had originally been established by the wall's trajectory, he decided to build a new wall whose serpentine course deferred to the trees by winding among them. The maples and oaks that affected the wall's form will ultimately determine its fate, for at a certain point their growth will dislodge the carefully laid stones.

Once the wall has emerged from the trees, it tapers and falls into a nearby pond. It then emerges from the other side of the pond, breaks for an intersecting road, and continues its "walk" uphill, stopping only at the outer edge of the Art Center's property. The wall's full 2,278-foot length, developed during the course of its construction, resulted from its internal energy and drive. From one end, the wall rises gradually from the ground, while the opposite approach presents an overall, breathtaking view of the compressed composition as it snakes through the trees and then releases its force into a straight path across an open field. Seasonal changes in light and in the density of the foliage also affect the wall's appearance. In the full bloom of summer, it is shielded from distant views and appears, unannounced, as one approaches. But in early spring and fall one can see its lateral expanse from afar. The light green of early spring and the red and orange tones of fall filter the light and color the stones anew. The character of the *Storm King Wall* evolved through an organic process; it is thoroughly melded with its site.

While Goldsworthy conceived the *Storm King Wall* and supervised its construction, the dry wall structure was built by an experienced, specialized team of British "wallers," using more than 1,500 tons of fieldstone gathered from the property. They explained exactly what kinds of stone to look for: chunky foundation stones, a variety for the wall's midsection, large "through stones" and flatter cap stones for the top layer, which intentionally blends with the structure as a whole. While the original stone wall probably marked the edge of a farmer's land, the new wall, which crosses a pond and two paths, is not an enclosure or a boundary marker. The flowing, linear structure claims the site as its own. Artistic inspiration once again brought an all-but-unnoticed area into high relief. The *Storm King Wall* (1997–98) is a playful yet magnificent sculpture, as well as a popular destination in a location from which new views of other works can be enjoyed.

[Text continues on page 190.]

OPPOSITE
A cross section of *Storm King Wall* is revealed where it comes to a halt to allow for a dirt road, a remnant of the farm that had once existed here.

ABOVE
One of Andy Goldsworthy's wallers in 1997 placing top stones on *Storm King Wall.* The only tools used by the wallers during the entire process were shovels and hammers.

PAGES 180–183
The *Storm King Wall* in 1999, through the progressing seasons.

Seen in the height of fall color, Andy Goldsworthy's *Storm King Wall* descends into a pond, but rises once again on the western bank from which it travels straight uphill to the New York State Thruway.

At the center of the eastern section of *Storm King Wall* its meandering course becomes deeply compressed; it seems to slow down in order to honor each tree in its path.

FOLLOWING TWO PAGES
The transparency of winter brings the form of *Storm King Wall* into strong relief.

The Art Center offers a range of experiences for visitors. In some areas one encounters a number of masterworks, but these monumentally scaled sculptures, such as Mark di Suvero's 65-foot-high *Pyramidian* (1986/98), are balanced by smaller, more intimate, and witty sculptures, including Charles Simonds's clay dwellings of the "Little People" (1981), nestled in two museum building windows facing the patio. Modestly scaled sculptures, such as John Newman's *Wit's End* (1988–89), also benefit from long vistas at the Art Center. This knotted sculpture, with its aluminum outer surface and partially shadowed interior, carries visually to distant locations, beckoning the curious to view its complex forms at close range.

The varied topography at Storm King yields many unexpected surprises. Smaller sculptures are often nestled in the woods, placed so that each encounter is a discovery. Some of the most important works in the collection can be discovered only by taking a walk away from the museum building, which today houses galleries for seasonal exhibitions. Some walking trails simply offer a peaceful respite from the world, as they were deliberately designed to include no art at all.

Nam June Paik's *Waiting for UFO* (1992) is a three-part, nontraditional poetic work incorporating elements for which the artist is famous, including broken television sets and the image of the Buddha. The commissioned sculpture has no single focus or narrative; it depends for its meaning on the gradual encounter of the viewer with its three distinctly sited parts.

Every day visitors walking away from the museum building discover the sculpture of a woman placed in the pachysandra. It is Saul Baizerman's unique, hand-hammered, copper *Aphrodite* acquired in 1980, a figure that draws its inspiration from the past but redefines classical beauty in contemporary terms. Created between 1940 and 1948, this is the oldest work in the Storm King collection.

A walk to the north trail rewards the visitor with mesmerizing views of the gently rotating *Sea Change* (1996) by the British sculptor George Cutts. Two tall, slender stainless-steel tubes anchored to a motorized stainless-steel disk turn slowly, creating the impression of fluid movement. This lyrical, kinetic stainless-steel composition evokes the currents and waves of the sea experienced by the artist while scuba diving.

The collection also includes Conceptual works that derive their meaning from the Art Center's history and philosophical framework. The French artist Daniel Buren walked around the grounds for many hours before deciding on his Conceptual project, titled *Sit down* (1998). He designed a group of fifteen cubic benches, painted with his signature bands of white alternating with a dark color, meant to be set in clusters at strategic, but changing, locations around the park. Each bench is clearly visible from afar, inviting visitors to walk to it and enjoy a rejuvenating rest.

[Text continues on page 199.]

OPPOSITE
Empty television sets, plastic flowers, and cast bronze and stone figures—sometimes of the Buddha—turn up enigmatically when a visitor comes upon two of the three installations of Nam June Paik's *Waiting for UfO.*

ABOVE
Elements of Paik's *Waiting for UFO* include bronze casts of the artist's face.

ABOVE
Of all the works in the Art Center's collection, Saul Baizerman's *Aphrodite* is one of the most traditional, but its surprising placement makes encountering it an entirely fresh experience.

OPPOSITE
The motorized, slowly rotating stems of *Sea Change*, by George Cutts, engage in a fascinating and soothing dance.

The striped, geometric object in the gorge of Moodna Creek has a welcome function for Art Center visitors who would like a place to sit down; the fifteen-part work by Daniel Buren is, in fact, titled *Sit down*.

When John Knight surveyed the Art Center landscape, he came to a very different concept, one centered on the distinctive single-unit water tower of the nearby Star Expansion Company. Knight proposed that the Art Center use a high-powered telescope to view the water tower, conceptually annexing the object to the collection. When Ralph E. Ogden and H. Peter Stern had installed the water tower in 1958, they envisioned the monumentally scaled structure (over 100 feet high) as more than a purely utilitarian object. The cost was double that of an ordinary water tower. In retrospect, it was their first aesthetic endeavor. For Knight, more than forty years later, it symbolizes a particularly modern relationship between economics, philanthropy, and aesthetics, one that has led to the creation of various important art museums. The Art Center has traditionally maintained consciousness of its surrounding areas, incorporating the Hudson Highlands as integral to the display of sculpture. Knight's project, titled *87°*, adapts this idea to a monumental but human-made object in the Art Center's wider environment, thereby both challenging and enriching our institution.

In the permanent collection of sculpture at the Storm King Art Center, work made since the mid-twentieth century predominates. Most of the sculptures on view are large and easily seen across long distances, taking advantage of the Art Center's most important resource—space. Sculptures must fit into both the landscape and the collection. Most works do not require formal settings, for the tone of the Art Center landscape is open and informal. The preponderance of works are constructed of durable rather than ephemeral materials, allowing them to remain outdoors. Conservation and maintenance have been crucially important since the first sculpture purchases were made in the early 1960s. Outdoor collections present unique challenges that must be addressed in order to protect the physical integrity of the sculptures for generations to come.

The sculpture collection at Storm King Art Center has changed significantly since the early years. The Art Center began to work toward the integration of sculpture and landscape under the watchful eyes of Ralph E. Ogden in the early 1970s and has refined this goal as the institution's mission since 1974 under the direction of H. Peter Stern. The Storm King Art Center continues to develop as an organic entity. There are a variety of spaces on the property that can accommodate additional sculptures into the harmonious balance of art and nature. However, the historic placement of the collection's landmark sculptures—including those by Alexander Calder, Mark di Suvero, Louise Nevelson, and Isamu Noguchi—and the integrity of long vistas will be protected in perpetuity.

OPPOSITE
The first aesthetic endeavor of Ralph E. Ogden and H. Peter Stern was the erection of this attractive (and rather costly) factory water tower—making it, in effect, an early anticipation of the Storm King Art Center.

ABOVE
The water tower of Star Expansion Company is visible just above the telescope in this photograph; John Knight's project, titled *87°*, brings the distant tower into the experience of visiting the Art Center.

Artists' Biographies

By Marie Busco, Ursula Lee, and Joan Pachner

MAGDALENA ABAKANOWICZ

Born 1930, Falenty, near Warsaw, Poland; lives in Warsaw. Abakanowicz is one of the most prominent sculptors to deal with existential and humanist issues in the last thirty years. She established her reputation in 1970s and 1980s with abstract and figurative sculptures molded with unusual materials, including burlap, flax, horsehair, and wool. Many of Abakanowicz's works, such as the famous *Backs* (1976–81), are composed of shell-like shapes suggesting body fragments. Their meaning is rooted in the atrocities she witnessed during World War II. As the adolescent child of an aristocratic Polish family, she had her life irrevocably fractured, but the reference in her work to barbarity is universal. Since the late 1980s Abakanowicz has cast numerous works in bronze, while she has created others, such as *War Games* (1987–93), from stripped trunks of large trees. *Sarcophagi in Glass Houses* is a unique work consisting of four large, nineteenth-century oak molds formerly used for casting turbine engines. She removed the painted surface of each mold, exposing its underlying abstract form, and subsequently enclosed each object in its own glass and iron framework. Like many of her works, *Sarcophagi in Glass Houses* alludes to decay, loss, and mourning. Abakanowicz has been commissioned to make many important environmental works; installations including more than eighty solo exhibitions have been shown worldwide. —MB

SELECTED REFERENCES: *Magdalena Abakanowicz. Les sarcophages* (Rennes; Musée des Beaux-Arts, Rennes, 1988); Michael Brenson, "Survivor Art," *The New York Times Magazine*, November 29, 1992, pp. 47–54; Barbara Rose, *Magdalena Abakanowicz* (New York: Harry N. Abrams, Inc., 1994).

Sarcophagi in Glass Houses, 1989
Wood, glass, and iron
8'6½" x 17'2½" x 143'3" (overall)
Gift of the artist
1994.2.a–d

SIAH ARMAJANI

Born 1939, Teheran, Iran; lives in Minnesota, where he emigrated in 1960. Armajani is renowned for large-scale, interactive works that merge sculpture with architecture. He borrows forms and materials from vernacular American architecture to make metaphoric structures that can be used as gathering places. Armajani made his first large-scale bridge sculpture in 1968 and, in 1975, began his Dictionary for Building series, in which architectural elements are presented in a skewed form, anticipating his later works. His sculptures owe a debt to Russian Constructivism and reflect his own "modernist populist" philosophy. In *Gazebo for Two Anarchists*, Armajani created a symbolic environment of constricted spaces for the viewer to enter, physically and psychologically, and meditate on incarceration and freedom. —MB

SELECTED REFERENCES: *Siah Armajani. Contributions anarchistes* (Nice: Villa Arson, 1994); *Siah Armajani. Recent Work* (Mountainville, New York: Storm King Art Center, 1993).

Gazebo for Two Anarchists: Gabriella Antolini and Alberto Antolini, 1992
Steel, painted blue-green, white, and black, and wood
6'3" x 9'5" x 20"
Gift of The Brown Foundation, Inc., the Ralph E. Ogden Foundation, Inc. and by exchange, Cynthia Hazen Polsky, donations in memory of Elizabeth Collens, the Joseph H. Hazen Foundation Purchase Fund, and an anonymous foundation
1992.2

ALICE AYCOCK

Born 1946, Harrisburg, Pennsylvania; lives in New York City. Aycock became fascinated by architecture at an early age when she took an interest in her father's construction business. She is an environmental artist celebrated for fantastic, sophisticated constructions that draw inspiration from wide-ranging sources including archaeology, science, astrology, and the Cabala. She is particularly concerned with systems of explaining and ordering the world. During the late 1970s and early 1980s, Aycock's work evolved from wooden mazes to threatening, but nonfunctional, mechanistic structures. Her interest in metaphysical issues dates from about 1980. The steeped bowl forms of *Three-Fold Manifestation II* evoke ancient Roman amphitheaters; the artist has also cited the influence of a Walter Gropius theater design and Leonardo da Vinci's drawings of swirling water. The intricate spiraling design suggests the helix of DNA. —MB

SELECTED REFERENCES: *Alice Aycock, Retrospective of Projects and Ideas, 1972–1983* (Württembergischer Kunstverein, 1983); *Complex Visions. Sculpture and Drawings by Alice Aycock* (Mountainville, New York: Storm King Art Center, 1990).

Three-Fold Manifestation II, 1987
Steel, painted white
29'3" x 14" x 12'
Gift of the artist
1987.1

SAUL BAIZERMAN

Born 1889, Vitebsk, Russia (now Belarus); died in 1957. Baizerman settled in New York City in 1911. He revitalized the classical nude figure with evocative hammered copper reliefs. He first discovered the expressive power of the direct metal technique when he made a series of small bronzes in the 1930s. Eventually he conceived figures on a more heroic scale and gave them mythological titles to suggest a universal, timeless quality. Many of his works, such as *Aphrodite*, were intended as metaphors for emotion or the forces of nature. He taught sculpture, drawing, and anatomy at the Baizerman Art School in New York City from 1934 to 1940. Baizerman received grants and awards from the Pennsylvania Academy of the Fine Arts and the Guggenheim Foundation between 1949 and 1952. —MB

SELECTED REFERENCES: Melissa Dubakis, *Vision of Harmony. The Sculpture of Saul Baizerman* (Redding Ridge, Connecticut: Black Swan Books, 1989); Carl Goldstein, "The Sculpture of Saul Baizerman," *Arts Magazine*, Sept. 1976, pp. 121–25; *Saul Baizerman* (Minneapolis: Walker Art Center, 1953).

Aphrodite, ca. 1940–48
Hammered copper
14" x 8' x 30"
Gift of the Ralph E. Ogden Foundation, Inc.
1980.6

DANIEL BUREN

Born 1938 in France; lives in Paris. Buren was a member of the B.M.P.T. group (Daniel Buren, Olivier Mosset, Michel Parmentier, and Niele Toroni), which in 1967 responded to the crisis in French art and modern art in general and began to embrace American Minimal and Conceptual art. Since the late 1960s Buren's visual signature has been a 3·-inch-wide (8.7-cm-wide) white stripe alternating with a dark color, which he superimposes onto the spatial organization of a given site, playing off the given order, thereby amplifying the viewer's sense of place. Buren's projects are always shaped by particular political and physical situations. The benches that constitute *Sit down* are not separate sculptures but are visually linked to one another as they punctuate the terrain they inhabit. The inherent tension between their aesthetic presence and their function creates an intentional ambiguity that is particularly resonant at Storm King. —UL

SELECTED REFERENCES: *Daniel Buren, Achtung!, Texte 1967–1991*, ed. Gerti Fietzek and Gudrun Inboden (Dresden/Basel: Verlag der Kunst, 1995); *Daniel Buren—Erscheinen-Scheinen-Verschwinden* (Düsseldorf: Kunstsammlung Nordrhein-Westfalen, 1996); Daniel Buren, *Les Escrits (1965–1990)*, ed. Jean-Marc Poinsot, vol. 1–3 (Bordeaux: CAPC, Musée d'art Contemporain de Bordeaux, 1991).

Sit down, 1998
Marine plywood, painted green and white
(a–j). 17¼ x 17¼ x 53`"
(k–o). 17¼ x 17¼ x 17¼"
Gift of the Ralph E. Ogden Foundation, Inc.
1998.2.a–o

ALEXANDER CALDER

Born 1898, Lawton, Pennsylvania; died 1976. Calder is renowned as a pioneer of abstract sculpture and as the creator of the first mobiles. The son and grandson of sculptors, he studied mechanical engineering before he attended the Art Students League in New York. His artistic sensibility was formed in Paris during the 1920s, under the influence of Joan Miró and Paul Klee, who, at first, inspired the whimsical wire-and-wood animal figures that evolved into Calder's famous *Circus*. His mature works combine Constructivist methods and Surrealist, often biomorphic imagery. Calder began to make abstract constructions after a visit to Piet Mondrian's studio in 1930. Two years later, he conceived his first mobiles, which were given their name by Marcel Duchamp. Jean Arp, in response to Duchamp, christened Calder's motionless painted metal constructions *stabiles*. During the 1960s and 1970s, these works gained colossal proportions, appropriate to the public sites for which they were often commissioned. *The Arch* is one of the last large-scale works that Calder completed before his death. It was fabricated at Segre Iron Works in Waterbury, Connecticut, and assembled and painted at Storm King, following the artist's instructions. —MB

SELECTED REFERENCES: Jean Lipman, *Calder's Universe* (Philadelphia and New York: Running Press in cooperation with Whitney Museum of American Art, 1976); Joan M. Marter, *Alexander Calder* (New York: Cambridge University Press, 1991); Marla Prather, *Alexander Calder 1898–1976* (Washington, D.C.: National Gallery of Art, 1998).

The Arch, 1975
Steel, painted black
50' x 41'6" x 34'10"
Purchase Fund and gift of the Ralph E. Ogden Foundation, Inc.
1982.3

ANTHONY CARO

Born 1924, London, where he lives. Caro studied engineering at Cambridge University before entering the Royal Academy, London, in 1947. From 1951 to 1953 he worked as an assistant to Henry Moore, but Caro's own early works were crudely modeled expressionistic figures in the spirit of Jean Dubuffet, the French Art Brut artist. A Ford Foundation grant in 1959 supported his first trip to the United States, where he came under the influence of critic Clement Greenberg and artist Kenneth Noland and saw works by David Smith for the first time. Back in London, Caro changed his style and his means of production, creating abstract welded steel sculptures made from industrial materials. He returned to the United States in 1963 to teach at Bennington College in Vermont. His works of the 1960s are horizontally oriented, placed directly on the floor, and painted a uniform color. As illustrated in the low-slung, curvilinear *Reel*, they tend to float or hover above the ground. These works revolutionized British sculpture by directing it further into abstraction and freeing it from the pedestal. Caro exercised profound influence on a younger generation of sculptors when he taught at St. Martins School of Art, London, in the 1950s and 1960s. He had a retrospective exhibition at the Museum of Modern Art in New York in 1975. After the 1970s his works became more massive and monumental, a trend that continued into the next decade when he began working with found objects, such as chain links and buoys from marine dockyards, which he had cast into bronze and which he then welded together. In the case of *Bitter Sky*, he moderated the mass of these objects by pairing them with delicate gray sheets of steel. In recent years Caro has made both abstract constructed sculpture and figural bronzes. —MB

SELECTED REFERENCES: Dieter Blume et al., *Anthony Caro: Catalogue raisonné*, 5 vols. (Cologne: Galerie Wentzel, 1982–1985); Giovanni Carandente, *Anthony Caro* (Milan: Fabbri Editori, 1992); Terry Fenton, *Anthony Caro* (New York: Rizzoli, 1986); William Rubin, *Anthony Caro* (New York: Museum of Modern Art, New York, 1975); Phyllis Tuchman, "An Interview with Anthony Caro," *Art in America*, Oct. 1984, pp. 146–53; Diane Waldman, *Anthony Caro* (New York: Abbeville Press, 1982).

Reel, 1964
Steel, painted red
34• " x 9'3" x 40"
Gift of the Ralph E. Ogden Foundation, Inc.
1970.5

Bitter Sky, 1983
Unpainted steel and steel, painted gray and brown
7'10" x 7'9" x 60"
Gift of James H. Ottaway, Jr., The Horace W. Goldsmith Foundation, and the Ralph E. Ogden Foundation, Inc.
1989.1

GEORGE CUTTS

Born 1938, Rugby, England; lives in Sussex. His sculpture is influenced by his experience at the Goole Shipyard, where he worked (1952–55) before attending the Doncaster School of Art (1955–57) and the Royal College of Art in London (1957–60). The motorized tall and slender steel tubes of *Sea Change* were inspired by the fluid movement of sea currents Cutts observed while scuba diving. Their undulating motion resembles that of large seaweed swaying to and fro and is timed to calm and tranquilize the viewer.

Cutts taught for many years at the Royal College of Art and the Royal Academy Schools, among other institutions, but has worked full-time as a sculptor since 1983. —UL

SELECTED REFERENCES: *British Contemporary Sculpture at Goodwood 1996–97* (Goodwood, Sussex: The Hat Hill Sculpture Foundation, 1996).

Sea Change, 1996
Stainless steel
25' high
Gift of the Ralph E. Ogden Foundation, Inc., The Horace W. Goldsmith Foundation, and the Margaret T. Morris Foundation
1998.4

MARK DI SUVERO

Born 1933, Shanghai, China; lives in New York City. He was raised in the Far East and California, where he emigrated in 1941. In 1957 he moved to New York, where, under the impact of Abstract Expressionism, he soon began to create rugged wood assemblages, which were first exhibited in the fall of 1960 at the Green Gallery. An accident in the spring of 1960 left him confined to a wheelchair for nearly two years and partially impaired. With the help of assistants, he began to make towering sculptures from construction materials—wooden ties, I beams, steel cables, and scrap metal—which he initially salvaged from demolition sites. By 1967 he had arrived at his heroic gestural signature style. The bold calligraphy of his works sometimes evokes the paintings of Franz Kline, the Abstract Expressionist artist he admired most. In 1971, di Suvero moved to Europe for four years to protest the Vietnam War, which he condemned in some of his sculpture, notably *Mother Peace. Mon Pére, Mon Pére* commemorates his father, who died when the artist was living in France. In 1985 di Suvero made a studio out of an abandoned warehouse on the waterfront in Long Island City, Queens, across the East River from Manhattan. The pyramidal base of many of his sculptures became the subject of the grand *Pyramidian*, created initially in 1986 and finished by the artist at Storm King in 1998. Since the mid-1980s many works, such as the complex *Mozart's Birthday* (1989), have contained an increased number of visual elements, including a varied repertoire of flat circular shapes of various sizes and numerous acute angles created by the I beams. Recently the artist has experimented with incorporating different materials, such as burnished stainless steel and titanium, into his compositions.

In 1975 di Suvero became the first living artist to exhibit in the Tuileries Gardens in Paris. In the same year he had a large retrospective at the Whitney Museum of American Art in New York, which included outdoor works sited throughout the city. Since that time his works have enjoyed tremendous popularity, as well as critical acclaim, in the United States and abroad. In 1985 a twenty-five-year retrospective of his sculptures and drawings was held at the Storm King Art Center. His work of the next decade was also shown at Storm King in 1995 and 1996, along with his paintings, which had not previously been exhibited in the United States. Always a politically committed artist, di Suvero founded the Athena Foundation in 1977, an organization dedicated to bringing together the general public and the fine arts and to supporting artists in need. In 1985 he created Socrates Sculpture Park, built on what had been a garbage-strewn vacant lot in Long Island City, Queens, New York. —MB

SELECTED REFERENCES: Monroe Denton, "A catalogue raisonné of the sculpture of Mark di Suvero," 4 vols. (Ph.D. dissertation, City University of New York, 1994); James K. Monte, *Mark di Suvero* (New York: Whitney Museum of American Art, 1975); Gilbert Perlain, *Mark di Suvero: Retrospective 1959–1991* (Nice: Musée d'Art Moderne et d'Art Contemporain, 1991); Barbara Rose, *Mark di Suvero: New Sculpture* (Houston: Janie C. Lee Gallery, 1978); Barbara Rose et al., *Mark di Suvero* (Valencia: IVAM Centre Julio González, 1994); Irving Sandler, *Mark di Suvero at Storm King Art Center* (Mountainville, New York,

New York: Storm King Art Center in association with Harry N. Abrams, Inc., 1996).

Mon Père, Mon Père, 1973–75
Steel
35' x 40' x 40'4"
Gift of the Ralph E. Ogden Foundation, Inc.
1981.11

Mother Peace, 1969–70
Steel, painted orange
41'8" x 49'5" x 44'3"
Gift of the Ralph E. Ogden Foundation, Inc.
1981.12

Pyramidian, 1987/98
Steel
56 x 46 x 46'
Gift of the Ralph E. Ogden Foundation, Inc.
1998.3

Mozart's Birthday, 1989
Steel
23 x 40 x 40'
Gift of Maurice Cohen and Margo Cohen
2000.2

ANDY GOLDSWORTHY

Born 1956, Cheshire, England, and raised in Yorkshire; lives in Scotland. He began to study the patterns of nature as a teenager while working on farms outside Leeds. His earliest environmental pieces date from the late 1970s. He prefers to work in remote regions, using whatever materials are at hand, often arranging them into ephemeral site-specific works, which he records in his own photographs. His projects have taken him to isolated locations as distant as the Australian outback and the North Pole. Since the mid-1980s, Goldsworthy has also produced permanent works, notably stone walls. For the artist, walls are resonant structures that represent the physical expression of movement, because each stone has been physically moved from one place to another, where it settles in place over time. At Storm King, he took a fallen wall as a point of departure but has rebuilt it as a new structure with great sensitivity to the environment. Rather than cutting an aggressive line across the landscape, the centerpiece of Goldsworthy's wall weaves in and out among the trees that have grown along the course of the original wall. —MB

SELECTED REFERENCES: Terry Friedman and Andy Goldsworthy, eds., *Hand to Earth. Andy Goldsworthy Sculpture 1976–1990* (New York: Harry N. Abrams, Inc., 1990); Andy Goldsworthy, *Wall: At Storm King* (Harry N. Abrams, Inc., 2000); Andy Goldsworthy, *Sheepfolds* (London: Michael Hue-Williams Fine Art, n.d.); Lynn Macritchie, "Residency on Earth," *Art in America*, Apr. 1995, pp. 95ff.

Storm King Wall, 1997–98
Fieldstone
approx. 5' x 2,278'6" (overall)
Gift of the Ralph E. Ogden Foundation, Inc., Mr. and Mrs. Joel Mallin, Mrs. W. L. Lyons Brown, Jr., Mr. and Mrs. James H. Ottaway, Jr., the Margaret T. Morris Foundation, The Horace W. Goldsmith Foundation, the Hazen Fund, the Joseph H. Hazen Foundation, Inc., Mr. and Mrs. Ronald N. Romary, Ms. Wendy Schaffer, Mr. Ivan Gjaja, and an anonymous foundation
1998.1

EMILIO GRECO

Born 1913, Catania, Sicily; died 1995 in Rome where he had lived since 1943 and where his career as figurative sculptor unfolded. Greco gained national fame with his creation of a public monument to *Pinocchio* (1953–56) in Collodi, Italy, and the bronze doors for the medieval cathedral of Orvieto (1959–62). But the central theme of his work was the sensuous female nude. He produced numerous bathers, rendered in Mannerist poses with modern physiognomies and clothing. *Large Bather I* belongs to a group of twelve bathers (seven executed) that Greco hoped to place around a pool.

Greco taught sculpture at the Naples and Rome Academies of Art and was also elected member to numerous European academies. —UL

SELECTED REFERENCES: Bernhard Degenhart, *Emilio Greco* (Kunsthalle Bremen, 1959); J. P. Hodin, *Emilio Greco* (Greenwich, Connecticut: New York Graphic Society 1971).

Large Bather I, 1956
Bronze
6'11" x 18" x 28"
Gift of the Ralph E. Ogden Foundation, Inc.
1963.41

Seated Woman, 1961
Bronze
13' x 8¼ x 7½"
Gift of the Ralph E. Ogden Foundation, Inc.
1962.12

ROBERT GROSVENOR

Born 1937, New York City; lives on Long Island, New York. In the 1960s Grosvenor employed industrial materials to produce geometric forms that were, at first, associated by critics with Minimalist art. He was among the founders of the cooperative Park Place Gallery in 1962. His early works were included in key exhibitions that defined the movement, but they were often more complex than other Minimalist structures, with suggestions of illusionism and dramatic tension. He established a reputation for sleek gravity-defying works that seemed to float or project boldly into space through cantilevering. The long, low-slung bridge structure at Storm King is an important example of Grosvenor's early site-specific works. Conceived in 1970, and fabricated in 1974, the untitled sculpture has a gently curved silhouette that spreads across an expansive field, evoking the form of the mountains beyond. The horizontal orientation corresponds to that of his earthbound sculptures of the 1970s, which similarly relate to the contours of a landscape. Many of his works created since the 1980s resemble archaic, primitive shelters. —MB

SELECTED REFERENCES: *Robert Grosvenor* (Centre d'art Contemporain du Domaine de Kerguehennec, 1989); *Robert Grosvenor* (Bern: Kunsthalle, 1992).

Untitled, 1970
Weathering steel, painted black
10' x 212'5½" x 12"
Gift of the Ralph E. Ogden Foundation, Inc.
1974.2

BARBARA HEPWORTH

Born 1903, Wakefield, Yorkshire, England; died 1975. This prolific British sculptor, who created about 500 works during her lifetime, became renowned for abstract sculptures that are often pierced by a hole, a device she conceived in 1931. She sometimes painted the hollows or bound them with a cat's cradle of string or wire. Much of her work was inspired by the landscape of her native Yorkshire, and especially Cornwall, where she lived for more than thirty years. Early in her career, she fell under the influence of her fellow artist from Yorkshire, Henry Moore. (They had met in 1920 as students in Leeds.) In 1933 Hepworth married the painter Ben Nicholson, who was the impetus behind some of her most austere works (they divorced in 1951). During visits to Paris, Nicholson introduced her to Hans Arp and Constantin Brancusi, among other artists. After World War II her work changed, increasingly reflecting the rugged landscape around St. Ives, Cornwall, her home since 1939. *Forms in Movement (Pavan)* was among Hepworth's first experiments with cast bronze; it was named for a stately Renaissance dance. *Square Forms with Circles* exemplifies her later renewed interest in the regularized geometric forms that characterized her carvings of the 1930s. —MB

SELECTED REFERENCES: Penelope Curtis and Alan G. Wilkinson, *Barbara Hepworth: A Retrospective* (Liverpool & Toronto: Tate Gallery, Liverpool & the Art Gallery of Ontario, 1994); Matthew Gale and Chris Stephens, *Barbara Hepworth: Works in the Tate Gallery Collection and the Barbara Hepworth Museum St. Ives* (London: Tate Gallery Publishing, 1999); Alan G. Wilkinson, *Barbara Hepworth: Sculptures from the Estate* (New York: Wildenstein & Co., 1996).

Forms in Movement (Pavan), 1956 (cast 1967)
Bronze
29½ x 43 x 22"
Gift of the Ralph E. Ogden Foundation, Inc.
1968.70

Square Forms with Circles, 1963
Bronze
12' x 58" x 27¼"
Gift of the Ralph E. Ogden Foundation, Inc.
1969.14

ALFRED HRDLICKA

Born 1928 in Vienna, Austria, where he lives. Hrdlicka's sculptures are distinguished by powerful distortions of the human figure, epitomized by *Golgotha* (1963) at Storm King. When he was a student of Franz Wotruba's at the Vienna Academy (1953–57), he worked in the Cubist idiom that was popular at that time. A left-wing political activist, Hrdlicka also opposed the abstraction that dominated the art world after World War II. In preparation for his first exhibition in 1960, he secretly reworked some of his student pieces and created other sculptures that were essentially expressionistic in spirit. His sculptures evoke the pathos of Auguste Rodin's works, but their aggressive political content recalls the satirical caricatures of the German artists George Grosz and Otto Dix. Although Hrdlicka is not religious, he has employed traditional Christian themes such as martyrdom to express his passionate socialist ideals. His major sculptures include the *Friedrich Engels Monument* (1976) for the city of Wuppertal and the *Renner Memorial* (1967), which deals with the issue of Austrian anti-Semitism.

Hrdlicka has taught at the International Summer Academy, Salzburg (1963), the Stuttgart Academy (1971 and 1975), the Hamburg College of Fine Arts (1973), and the Berlin Academy of Fine Arts (1986). In 1978 he became a corresponding member of the Art Academy of the German Democratic Republic. —UL

SELECTED REFERENCES: Alfred Hrdlicka, "Hrdlicka über sich selbst" (Hanover: Kestner-Gesellschaft, 1974); Klaus Klemp and Peter Weiermair, eds., *Alfred Hrdlicka. Sculptures, Drawings, Prints, 1945–1997* (Frankfurt am Main: Frankfurter Kunstverein; Kilchberg/Zurich: Edition Stemmle, 1997); Michael Lewin, *Alfred Hrdlicka. Das Gesamtwerk*, 3 vols., (Vienna and Zurich: Europa Verlag, 1987–89).

Golgotha, 1963
Marble
7'3¼" x 23" x 19½"
Gift of the Ralph E. Ogden Foundation, Inc.
1963.42

PATRICIA JOHANSON

Born 1940, New York City; lives in upstate New York. An innovative environmental artist since 1969, she has also been acclaimed for her efforts in ecology and urban renewal. Her primary goal is to bring people and the landscape together by involving the viewer as an active participant in her works. Johanson often leaves much of the natural habitat untouched and modifies a site only slightly to create poetic spaces for the spectator to experience. *Nostoc II* is one of her earliest site-specific ecological projects. She introduced boulders and stones from a different part of the Art Center and arranged them in a deliberate pattern. From above, the arrangement of the rocks resembles the molecular structures of the blue-green algae from which the title is derived. —MB

SELECTED REFERENCES: Debra Bricker Balken and Lucy Lippard, *Patricia Johanson: Drawings and Models for Environmental Projects, 1969–1986* (Pittsfield, Massachusetts: Berkshire Museum, 1987); Barbara Matilsky, *Fragile Ecologies. Contemporary Artists' Interpretations and Solutions* (New York: Queens Museum of Art, 1992).

Nostoc II, 1975
Stone
30" x 49'3" x 40'9"
Gift of the Ralph E. Ogden Foundation, Inc.
1975.69

MENASHE KADISHMAN

Born 1932 in Tel Aviv, where he lives. His sculptures of the 1960s are Minimalist in style, some employing glass so as to appear to defy gravity and merge with the environment. *Suspended*, at Storm King, represents a continuation of these concerns. The cantilevered metal sculpture is alluring, in part, because the tilted structure has no obvious means of support. During the 1970s, Kadishman began to base his work more directly on natural themes, as exemplified by *Eight Positive Trees* (1977), in which steel silhouettes of trees form a counterpoint to the real foliage in the landscape. The forms were cut out from his *Negative Trees* (Israel Museum, Jerusalem), which was exhibited at the Venice Biennale in 1978. Since the 1980s, biblical themes have figured importantly in his work. —UL

SELECTED REFERENCES: *Menashe Kadishman: sculpture and drawings* (London: Annely Juda Fine Art, 1992); *Menashe Kadishman: small sculpture* (New York: Nora Haime Gallery, 1990); Peter Selz, "Menashe Kadishman: Planting Trees, Making Sculpture," *Arts*, Dec. 1976, pp. 95–97.

Eight Positive Trees, 1977
Weathering steel
14'5• " x 46' x 25'3" (overall)
Gift of Muriel and Philip I. Berman
1985.2.a–h

Suspended, 1977
Weathering steel
23' x 33' x 48"
Gift of Muriel and Philip I. Berman
1985.3

JOHN KNIGHT

Born 1945, Hollywood, California; lives in New York City. Since the late 1960s Knight has used various means to create a dialogue between an artwork and its site, often highlighting the subject of patronage. While he has used video and slide projections in his indoor mixed-media installations since late 1969, the outdoor project at the Storm King Art Center employs only a high-power telescope, through which a visitor can view the top of a silver colored, single-unit water tower (more than 100 feet high). The water tower is located about a mile south of the Art Center, on the grounds of the former Star Expansion Company, the company previously owned by Ralph E. Ogden and H. Peter Stern. The success of Star Expansion enabled Ogden and Stern to realize their vision for the Storm King Art Center. Moreover, Star Expansion originally owned much of the land that currently belongs to the Art Center. The single-unit water tower itself, erected in 1958, exemplifies Ogden and Stern's early aesthetic bent, as they justified its rather high cost on the strength of its visual appeal. Knight has conceptually incorporated the utilitarian object into the Storm King Art Center's collection. The water tower has been appropriated as a work of art and used as a visual sign referring to the Art Center's founders. He has used a bare minimum of means to stress the essential relationship between the Art Center today and the industrial roots of its philanthropic patrons. —JP

SELECTED REFERENCES: Anne Goldstein and Anne Rorimer, *Reconsidering the Object of Art: 1965–1975* (Los Angeles: The Museum of Contemporary Art, 1995); *John Knight* (Chicago: The Renaissance Society at the University of Chicago, 1983); *John Knight–Haim Steinbach* (Brussels: Palais des Beaux-Arts, 1991).

87°, 1997–99
Gift of the Ralph E. Ogden Foundation, Inc.
1999.1

SOL LEWITT

Born 1928, Hartford, Connecticut, where he lives. LeWitt is often associated with Minimalism, though he prefers the term *Conceptual art*, because his works stress the primacy of the thought process. He started his career as a painter and graphic designer for the architect I. M. Pei. In 1963 he made his first constructions, reliefs, and boxlike forms. Two years later, he conceived the earliest of the geometric modular works with which he is identified. In keeping with his intellectual aims, LeWitt restricted himself to austere materials, such as wood or steel, and employed neutral surfaces, usually white enamel. As exemplified by *Five Modular Units*, these objects are based on the repetition of identical cubic forms. During the 1960s and early 1970s he sometimes created elaborate variations of these units, usually by means of mathematical calculations. LeWitt and other Conceptual artists emphasized idea over execution so that assistants or others could carry out the projected designs. This principle was applied to his influential wall drawings, which he began to produce in 1968. Since the 1980s, the colors of LeWitt's works have become more lush and their complex installations increasingly filled with irregular shapes as the artist explores an expanded spatial and psychological realm. —MB

SELECTED REFERENCES: Yve-Alain Bois, "Sum and the Parts," *Artforum*, Feb. 2000, pp.92–97; Gary Garrels, *Sol LeWitt: A Retrospective* (New Haven: Yale University Press, 2000); *Sol LeWitt* (New York: Museum of Modern Art, 1978); *Sol LeWitt, structures 1962–1993* (Oxford: Museum of Modern Art, 1993).

Five Modular Units, 1971
Steel, painted white
63" x 63" x 24'3"
Gift of the Ralph E. Ogden Foundation, Inc.
1971.20

Maquette for Five Modular Units, 1966
Wood painted white
5` x 24 x 5"
1971.23

ALEXANDER LIBERMAN

Born 1912, Kiev, Russia (now Ukraine); died 1999, Miami, Florida. Known equally for his work as the art director and, later, editorial director at Condé Nast publications and for the vividly painted tubular sculptures that adorn many civic plazas and sculpture parks, Liberman was also an accomplished photographer. In 1925, he and his family emigrated to Paris, where he studied painting and began his career in design. Liberman moved to the United States in 1941. His interest in sculpture was stimulated when he learned welding techniques in 1959. Philip Johnson commissioned Liberman's first public sculpture for the New York World's Fair in 1964. From that time he continued to work on a monumental scale and was noted for his use of industrial materials—often old, rusted steel boilers and storage tanks that he would sandblast and paint at his rural Connecticut outdoor studio. *Adonai* is one of only a few early works in which the components were used in their natural rusted state. Liberman titled this sculpture *Adonai*, a Hebrew word for God, following a trip to the great Gothic cathedral in Chartres, France. Its mock-classical vocabulary of falling columns evokes architectural models. The tubular elements of *Iliad* and *Adam* are sliced to make the elliptical forms that dominate his oeuvre. Sometimes these elements are cantilevered to suggest movement, particularly upward thrust, as demonstrated in the flamboyant *Iliad*. —MB

SELECTED REFERENCES: Carter Ratcliff, "Alexander Liberman at Storm King," *Art in America*, Nov./Dec. 1977, pp. 100–101; Barbara Rose, *Alexander Liberman* (New York: Abbeville Press, 1981).

Adam, 1970
Steel, painted orange
28'6" x 24' x 29'6"
Gift of the Ralph E. Ogden Foundation, Inc.
1974.29

Adonai, 1970–71 (refabricated 2000)
Steel
29'6" x 63' x 52'8"
Gift of the Ralph E. Ogden Foundation, Inc.
1974.31

Iliad, 1970–71
Steel painted orange
36' x 54'7" x 19'7"
Gift of the Ralph E. Ogden Foundation, Inc.
1981.10

Untitled, 1964
Bronze
9 x 5½ x 3' "
Gift of the Betty Parsons Foundation
1984.9

HENRY MOORE

Born 1898, Castleford, West Yorkshire, England; died 1986. Moore is regarded as the most important British sculptor of the twentieth century and one of the masters of modern sculpture. He is renowned for abstract figures that evoke natural landscape forms. Moore carved his first reclining female figure in 1927. He was influenced in the early part of his career by African and pre-Columbian art and later by the Surrealist works of Pablo Picasso and Hans Arp. Although he believed in direct carving and "truth to materials," he began to have his work cast in bronze or lead in the late 1930s. After World War II, increasing fame led to numerous commissions and large-scale cast bronzes. From the 1950s until the end of his life Moore was in great demand as a sculptor of public monuments. In 1948 he represented Britain at the first postwar Venice Biennale and was awarded the grand prize for sculpture. Much of his work became increasingly abstract, as can be seen in *Reclining Connected Forms*. In this horizontal sculpture, one form is enclosed within another, abstractly suggesting a mother and child group or an infant in the womb. —MB

SELECTED REFERENCES: Alan Bowness, ed., *Henry Moore: Complete Sculpture* (London: Lund Humphries, 1977, reprinted 1991); *Henry Moore: From the Inside Out* (Munich and New York: Prestel, 1996); *Henry Moore: Sixty Years of His Art* (New York: The Metropolitan Museum of Art, 1983); H. J. Seldis, *Henry Moore in America* (New York: Praeger, 1973).

Reclining Connected Forms, 1969
Bronze
36' " x 7'4" x 52"
Gift of the Ralph E. Ogden Foundation, Inc.
1971.22

LOUISE NEVELSON

Born 1899, Kiev, Russia (now Ukraine); died 1988, New York City. Nevelson emigrated with her family to Rockland, Maine, in 1905; she moved to New York City in 1920. She is celebrated for her evocative shadowbox reliefs and unique wall sculptures. Her earliest abstract wood constructions, which incorporated found objects, date from the mid-1940s. In 1956 she started to paint her works black, which became her signature color. A year later, she began to enclose wood reliefs in boxes and made her initial wall pieces. Her first experiments with steel date from 1966. Nevelson frequently combined elements from existing works to create a new composition. In *City on the High Mountain*, she connected parts of two separate projects from the 1970s—one curvilinear, the other more rectilinear—with found and created metal elements, creating a 10-foot model of a new sculpture, which was then enlarged to a height of more than 20 feet. The title of the piece at Storm King—*City on the High Mountain*—was inspired by its setting. —MB

SELECTED REFERENCES: Arnold Glimcher, *Louise Nevelson* (New York: Praeger, 1972); Harriet Senie, *Nevelson at Purchase: The Metal Sculpture* (Neuberger Museum, State University of New York at Purchase, 1977).

City on the High Mountain, 1983
Weathering steel, painted black
20'6" x 23' x 13'6"
Purchase Fund
1984.4

Diminishing Reflection XXV, 1966
Wood painted black, and Plexiglas
17 x 17½ x 6"
Gift of Cynthia Hazen Polsky
1984.5

JOHN NEWMAN

Born 1952 in New York City, where he lives. Newman is an abstract sculptor and printmaker with roots in Minimalism. His scientific interests in topology, physics, and astronomy, as well as linguistics, prompted a new, more complex direction in his work in the 1980s. Newman's fascination with topological equivalence—the transformation of one shape into another by bending and pulling—resulted in the deformation and torsion of his sculptural surfaces, while evoking intriguing associations. The verbal puzzle of the title *Wit's End* is compounded by the difference in structure of its two cones, which are bound within a taut, giant coil. Newman treated the aluminum as if it had been exposed to a wrenching, twisting force. —UL

SELECTED REFERENCES: *John Newman: Sculpture and Drawings* (San Francisco: John Berggruen Gallery, 1991); *John Newman, Sculpture and Works on Paper* (Fort Wayne, Indiana: Fort Wayne Museum of Art, 1993); Nancy Princenthal, *John Newman's Recent Prints, Drawings and Sculpture* (Mount Kisco, New York: Tyler Graphics Ltd., 1990).

Wit's End, 1988–89
Aluminum
46½" x 10'9" x 64"
Gift of the family of Joseph H. Hazen in honor of his 90th birthday.
1989.2

ISAMU NOGUCHI

Born 1904 in Los Angeles of mixed Japanese and American parentage; died 1988, New York City. Noguchi worked in the United States and Japan; his sculpture reflects an aesthetic synthesis of Eastern and Western cultures. From 1906 to 1917 he lived in Japan but was sent to America in 1918 to attend high school. While visiting Paris in 1927 (with funds from a Guggenheim Fellowship), he worked briefly as a studio assistant to Constantin Brancusi. Noguchi made abstract sculptures and portraits in the late 1920s and 1930s. In 1933 he created his first large-scale public project proposals, *Monument to Ben Franklin* and *Play Mountain*, and, in 1935, a stage set for Martha Graham's dance *Frontier*, initiating a collaboration that continued until 1966. Noguchi designed his first utilitarian object in 1937. This important aspect of his oeuvre later included lamps and a coffee table, many still in production today. He experimented with various materials through the 1940s. During World War II Noguchi voluntarily interned himself at a Japanese relocation camp in Poston, Arizona. A grant from the Bollingen Foundation supported his travels in Asia and Europe from 1949 to 1952; during this time Noguchi created his first environmental garden in Tokyo, Japan (completed 1952). In 1956 he worked on commissioned environmental projects in the United States and at UNESCO headquarters in Paris. In 1961 he established a studio in Long Island City, New York, which in 1985 became the Isamu Noguchi Garden Museum. In 1971 he established another studio on the island of Shikoku, Japan. A superb carver, Noguchi often refined his material to a highly finished state but was also fascinated by rough and broken surfaces.

Noguchi was a member of the American Academy of Arts and Sciences and received countless awards and medals. —UL

SELECTED REFERENCES: Bruce Altshuler, *Isamu Noguchi* (New York: Abbeville Press, 1994); Martin Friedman, *Noguchi's Imaginary Landscapes* (Minneapolis: Walker Art Center, 1978); Nancy Grove, *Isamu Noguchi: A Study of the Sculpture* (New York: Garland Publishing, 1985); Sam Hunter, *Isamu Noguchi* (New York: Abbeville, 1978); Isamu Noguchi, *The Isamu Noguchi Garden Museum* (New York: Abrams, 1987); Isamu Noguchi, *A Sculptor's World* (New York: Harper & Row, 1968).

Momo Taro, 1977–78
Granite
9' x 34'7" x 21'7" (overall)
Gift of the Ralph E. Ogden Foundation, Inc.
1978.4.a–i

NAM JUNE PAIK

Born 1932, Seoul, South Korea; lives in New York City. Paik is renowned as a pioneer video and performance artist and as a sculptor and writer. He emigrated first to Tokyo in 1952 and four years later to West Germany, where he became involved with the avant-garde music scene and collaborated with composer John Cage. He began to exploit television technology in his art as early as the 1960s. In 1963 he exhibited his earliest "electronic paintings," television sets with scrambled images. A year later, he moved to New York and associated with the neo-Dadaist Fluxus artists. In subsequent decades, he became famous for his installations of television sets filled with assorted objects, and of stacked video monitors displaying witty or dazzling abstract imagery. In his works, television often assumes a shrinelike role, as it does in modern society. *Waiting for UFO* is one of only a few works in which he arranged televisions sets and some of his favorite objects, notably seated Buddhas, in an actual landscape setting. —MB

SELECTED REFERENCES: J. G. Hanhardt, *Nam June Paik* (New York: Whitney Museum of American Art, 1982); J. G. Hanhardt, *The Worlds of Nam June Paik* (New York: Solomon R. Guggenheim Museum, 2000); Patricia Mellencamp, "The Old and the New. Nam June Paik," *Art Journal*, Winter 1995, pp. 41–47.

Waiting for UFO, 1992
Bronze, stone, plastic, and concrete (in three parts)
a. 24" x 10'7" x 15'
b. 6' x 20'2" x 20'2"
c. 41 x 28 x 30"
Gift of Cynthia Hazen Polsky, the Joseph H. Hazen Foundation, Inc., and the Ralph E. Ogden Foundation, Inc.
1992.3.a–c

JOSEPH PILLHOFER

Born 1929, Vienna, Austria. He maintains a studio in Vienna as well as in Mürzzuschlag, Styria (southeast Austria), where he was raised. He studied at the Graz Arts and Crafts School and, after 1945, continued at the Vienna Academy of Fine Arts as a pupil of Fritz Wotruba, the leading of Austrian postwar sculptor. He adopted a Cubist vocabulary after attending the Académie de la Grande Chaumière in Paris in 1950–51, where he studied with Ossip Zadkine and Henri Laurens. Pillhofer's carved *Man in the Quarry* (1960) and the cast bronze *Reclining Man* (1964) reflect their influence. Although he also developed a naturalistic figurative style, it is the abstract forms of *Archaic Stone* (1964) and *White En* (1965) that anticipate his work from the 1980s until the present day. Nevertheless, he continues to derive his inspiration from nature and the human form.

Pillhofer held teaching positions at the Academy of Fine Arts, Vienna, and the Arts and Crafts School, Graz. A recipient of important Austrian state prizes and awards, he also participated in many international exhibitions including the Venice Biennale, the Carnegie International, as well as the Musée Rodin exhibition of contemporary sculpture. He participated in sculpture symposia at the quarry of St. Margarethen in Austria (where Ralph E. Ogden first saw his work in the fall of 1960), Antwerp and Middleheim in the Netherlands, Montreal in Canada, and Soest in Germany. A selection of his work is permanently on view at the former Franciscan church of Mürzzuschlag in Styria. —UL

SELECTED REFERENCES: *Josef Pillhofer. Das Gestalthafte in der Nature* (Mürzzuschlag: Kulturreferat der Stadtgemeinde Mürzzuschlag, 1981); *Josef Pillhofer, Skulpturen und Collages* (Vienna: Österreichische Galerie, Oberen Belvedere, 1971); *Josef Pillhofer: Zeichnunben 1944–1991* (Vienna: Albertina, Graphische Sammlung, 1991–92).

Man in the Quarry, 1960
Limestone
8'5½" x 37" x 36"
Gift of the Ralph E. Ogden Foundation, Inc.
1961.4

Archaic Stone, 1964
Limestone
7' 7" x 21" x 16"
Gift of Joan O. Stern
1983.1

Dynamic Architecture, 1964
Limestone
24 x 14 x 12"
Gift of Joan O. Stern
1983.2

Reclining Man, 1964
Bronze
13 x 46 x 15"
Gift of Joan O. Stern
1983.3

White En, 1965
Marble
49½ x 19 x 20"
Gift of Margaret Hovenden Ogden
1978.19

GEORGE RICKEY

Born 1907, South Bend, Indiana, and raised in Scotland; lives in East Chatham, New York. Rickey, who is famous for his wind-driven kinetic sculptures of reflective stainless steel, made his first kinetic works out of glass in 1949. The imagery of his mobiles of the 1950s is primarily organic and evokes Alexander Calder's work, but by the 1960s his sculptures had become more geometric in form and Constructivist in conception. *Six Lines in a T* is among his earliest non-objective works, typical of the "classic" steel mobiles that emerged in the 1960s. By 1968 Rickey had extended his vocabulary to include solid planes and shallow boxlike shapes, as exemplified by *Two Planes Vertical-Horizontal II. Five Open Squares Gyratory, Gyratory* is a later, more complex piece, in which the forms rotate around the central stem, rather than in a linear path. —MB

SELECTED REFERENCES: Jörn Merkert and Ursula Prinz, eds., *George Rickey in Berlin 1967–1992* (Berlin: Museum für Moderne Kunst, Berlinishche Galerie, 1992); Nan Rosenthal, *George Rickey* (New York: Abrams, 1977); Reiko Tomii, *Between two continents: George Rickey, kinetic art and constructivism, 1949–1968* (Ph.D. dissertation, University of Texas at Austin, 1988).

Six Lines in a T, 1965–66/79
Stainless steel
10'8" x 6'6½" x 30½"
Gift of the Ralph E. Ogden Foundation, Inc.
1967.18

Two Planes Vertical-Horizontal II, 1970
Stainless steel
14'7 " x 10'5" x 6'3"
Gift of the Ralph E. Ogden Foundation, Inc.
1971.12

Five Open Squares Gyratory Gyratory, 1981
Stainless steel
9'4" x 6' x 42"
Gift of the artist and Joan O. Stern by exchange
1992.1

RICHARD SERRA

Born 1939, San Francisco; lives in New York City. In the late 1960s Serra became involved with process art, including video and filmmaking, through which he examined the performance of tasks in real time. *Pulitzer Piece: Stepped Elevation* (1970) in St. Louis, initiated a series of large outdoor urban and landscape works in which he used mass-produced industrial materials such as lead and steel plates. *Shift*, a topographical piece created for a private Canadian collector in 1971, presages *Schunnemunk Fork*, made twenty years later at the Storm King Art Center. A video documents the creation of *Shift*. The lengths of its wedged concrete shapes were determined by the maximum distance from which two people could keep each other in view while walking the undulating terrain. This approach provided a starting point for Serra's site-specific sculpture at Storm King, although eventually it evolved into a more expansive project encompassing views far beyond its 10-acre site. *Schunnemunk Fork* consists of four massive horizontal steel plates inserted into the landscape. As one walks through the spaces created by the sculptures, each straight-edged plate becomes a separate horizon. Their planar forms make variations in the terrain more obvious; they also intensify one's awareness of the undulating profiles of nearby Storm King and Schunnemunk Mountains. In the past decade, Serra has worked with massive plates of hot-rolled steel shaped into complex curves to create sculpture on an architectural scale that encloses and activates space.

Among Serra's numerous awards are a Yale Travel Fellowship (1964), a Fulbright Study Grant (1965), a Guggenheim Fellowship (1970), the Sculpture Award of Skowhegan School of Painting and Sculpture (1976), and the Wilhelm Lehmbruck Prize (1991). In 1983 he received an Honorable Fellowship of Bezaled Academy, Jerusalem, and in 1985 was made Chevalier dans l'Ordre des Arts et des Lettres by the French government. —UL

SELECTED REFERENCES: Richard Hoppe-Sailer and Mark Demming, *Richard Serra: Prints 1972–1988. Catalog Raisonné* (Berlin: Neuer Berliner Kunstverein, 1988); Hans Janssen, ed., *Richard Serra: drawings 1969–1990. Catalog Raisonné* (Bern: Benteli, 1990); Richard Koshalek and Julia Brown, *Richard Serra: sculpture 1985–1998* (Los Angeles: Museum of Contemporary Art, 1998).

Schunnemunk Fork, 1990–91
Weathering steel
a. 8' x 49'1" x 2½"
b. 8' x 35'1" x 2½"
c. 8' x 38'4" x 2½"
d. 8' x 54'4" x 2½"
Gift of the Ralph E. Ogden Foundation, Inc. by exchange, The Brown Foundation, Inc., and an anonymous foundation
1991.1.a–d

CHARLES SIMONDS

Born 1945 in New York City, where he lives. Simonds's dwellings for the "Little People" of an imaginary civilization seem to be archaeological remains of ancient lilliputian cities constructed of clay, bricks, and sticks. Whether small or large, his elaborate constructions symbolize the spirit of communal living through the ages, in tribal villages as well as in contemporary cities. They seem to refer to evolution as well as permanence, to the mythic past and to present living conditions. Simonds's expansive vision may also reflect the influence of Robert Smithson's contemporaneous monumental Earthworks. Since the mid-1990s he has created distorted figural compositions that focus on the artist's internal psyche.

Simonds was recipient of a National Endowment for the Arts grant as well as a New York State Council for the Arts grant in 1974. —UL

SELECTED REFERENCES: John Beardsley, "Hybrid Dreams," *Art in America*, Mar. 1995, pp. 92–97; *Charles Simonds* (Barcelona: Centro Cultural de la Fundacio La Caixa, 1994); *Charles Simonds* (Chicago: Museum of Contemporary Art, 1981); *Refuge* (Washington, D.C.: Corcoran Gallery of Art, 1988); *The Three Trees im Architekturmuseum in Basel* (Basel: Architekturmuseum, 1987).

Dwellings, 1981
Clay, pigment, ceramic bricks, and sticks
9½ x 13 x 10"
Purchased with the aid of funds from the National Endowment for the Arts and gift of the Ralph E. Ogden Foundation, Inc.
1981.3.1

Dwellings, 1981
Clay, pigment, ceramic bricks, and sticks
13 x 22½ x 10"
Purchased with the aid of funds from the National Endowment
of the Arts and gift of the Ralph E. Ogden Foundation, Inc.
1981.3.2

DAVID SMITH

Born 1906, Decatur, Indiana; died, 1965, Bennington, Vermont.
Although Smith began his career as a painter, he revolutionized
American sculpture in 1932 when, inspired by photographs
he had seen of welded assemblages by Pablo Picasso and Julio
González, he began to make welded metal sculptures from
discarded, found objects. While living in Brooklyn, New York,
Smith rented studio space from a small company called Terminal Iron Works Boiler-Tube Makers and Ship Deck Fitters. In
1940 he and his wife, the artist Dorothy Dehner, relocated to a
home they had owned since 1929 in the rural town of Bolton
Landing, near Lake George in New York State's Adirondack
Mountains. Smith's first fully mature work emerged in 1950
and 1951, when he was supported by grants from the Solomon
R. Guggenheim Foundation. Smith and Dehner divorced in
1952. He married Jean Freas in 1953, with whom he had two
daughters: Candida (born 1953) and Rebecca (born 1955).

He was renowned for large, openwork compositions that
created the effect of "drawing in space." From 1954 to 1957,
Smith also made numerous bronze sculptures, often by casting
found objects, then welding elements together to form unique
compositions. In 1958 he burnished unpainted, stainless steel
with a circular sander, creating painterly, brilliantly reflective
surfaces on works intended to be placed outdoors. This innova-
tion enabled him to ally sculpture with painting in new ways,
culminating with the monumental Cubi series (1961–65) and
the large, planar compositions made shortly before he died. In
the summer of 1962, he traveled to Italy for the fourth Festival
of Two Worlds in Spoleto. He intended to continue work with
stainless steel but was offered access to five abandoned facto-
ries and six assistants. Using a combination of found objects
and created shapes, he made twenty-seven sculptures during
his one-month stay. He shipped home crates of materials to
Bolton Landing, and beginning in December, he made the
Voltri-Bolton series. In February 1965, President Lyndon
Johnson appointed him to the National Council on the Arts.
On May 23, driving in Bennington, Vermont, his truck over-
turned; he died that night. He had been actively involved in
planning an upcoming retrospective at Los Angeles County
Museum that opened in November as "David Smith: A
Memorial Exhibition." —JP

SELECTED REFERENCES: E. A. Carmean, Jr., *David Smith*
(Washington, D.C.: National Gallery of Art, 1982); *The Fields of
David Smith* (Mountainville, New York, and New York: Storm
King Art Center and Thames & Hudson, 1999); Cleve Gray, ed.,
David Smith by David Smith (New York; Holt, Rinehart and
Winston, Inc., and London: Thames & Hudson, 1968; reprinted
London: Thames & Hudson, 1988); Rosalind E. Krauss,
Terminal Iron Works (Cambridge, Mass.: The MIT Press, 1971);
Rosalind E. Krauss, *David Smith: A Catalogue Raisonné* (New
York: Garland Publishers, 1977); Garnett McCoy, ed., *David
Smith* (New York: Praeger, 1973); Karen Wilkin, *David Smith*
(New York: Abbeville Press, 1984).

The Sitting Printer, 1954–55
Bronze
7'3" x 15¼" x 17"
Gift of the Ralph E. Ogden Foundation, Inc.
1967.9

Portrait of a Lady Painter, 1954; 1956–57
Bronze
64 x 59¼ x 12½"
Gift of the Ralph E. Ogden Foundation, Inc.
1967.7

The Iron Woman, 1954–58
Steel, painted light green
59 x 55 x 11"
Gift of the Ralph E. Ogden Foundation, Inc.
1967.5

Five Units Equal, 1956
Steel, painted light green
6'1‚ " x 16" x 14"
Gift of the Ralph E. Ogden Foundation, Inc.
1967.4

Personage of May, 1957
Bronze
71 x 31½ x 18½"
Gift of the Ralph E. Ogden Foundation, Inc.
1967.6

Study in Arcs, 1957
Steel, painted pink
11'9' 6½" x 36½"
Gift of the Ralph E. Ogden Foundation, Inc.
1967.10

Albany I, 1959
Steel, painted black
25 x 25¼ x 7‚ "
Gift of the Ralph E. Ogden Foundation, Inc.
1967.1

XI Books III Apples, 1959
Stainless steel
7'10" x 35" x 16‚ "
Gift of the Ralph E. Ogden Foundation, Inc.
1967.3

Raven V, 1959
Steel, and stainless steel
59 x 55 x 11"
Gift of the Ralph E. Ogden Foundation, Inc.
1967.8

Tanktotem VII, 1960
Steel, painted dark blue and white
7'½" x 37" x 14` "
Gift of the Ralph E. Ogden Foundation, Inc.
1967.11

Three Ovals Soar, 1960
Stainless steel
11'3½" x 31" x 23"
Gift of the Ralph E. Ogden Foundation, Inc.
1967.12

Volton XX, 1963
Steel
62½ x 34 x 29"
Gift of the Ralph E. Ogden Foundation, Inc.
1967.13

Becca, 1964
Steel
6'6" x 47½" x 23½"
Gift of the Ralph E. Ogden Foundation, Inc.
1967.2

KENNETH SNELSON

Born 1927, Pendelton, Oregon; lives in New York City. Snelson creates open structures with stainless-steel cables attached to stainless-steel pipes. His sculptures appear suspended in space; they are held together by the push and pull of their internal forces. Extending vertically or horizontally, they seem infinitely expandable and appear to defy gravity. Snelson associates his fascination with tension structures with his continuing search for an unchanging truth. The system was named *tensegrity* by Buckminster Fuller, who had been Snelson's teacher at Black Mountain College in North Carolina in the summers of 1948 and 1949; the term has passed into the vocabulary of engineering. The arched *Free Ride Home* (1974) exhibits a rare combination of strength and whimsy. It both melds with its environment and creates its own impression on the sky for viewers who lie on the grass and look up at the expansive form.

Snelson is a member of the American Academy and Institute of Arts and Letters and has received a DAAD Fellowship for Berlin Künstlerprogramm, as well as grants from the National Endowment of the Arts and the New York State Council on the Arts. —UL

SELECTED REFERENCES: Joelle Burrows, *Kenneth Snelson, the nature of structure* (New York: New York Academy of Sciences, 1989); Douglas G. Schultz and Howard N. Fox, *Kenneth Snelson, an exhibition* (Buffalo, New York: Albright-Knox Art Gallery, 1981); *Kenneth Snelson, sculptures* (New York: Maxwell Davidson Gallery, 1994).

Free Ride Home, 1974
Aluminum and stainless steel
30 x 60 x 60'
Gift of the Ralph E. Ogden Foundation, Inc.
1975.64

TAL STREETER

Born in 1934, Oklahoma City; lives in Verbank, New York. Early in his career, Streeter made linear black-painted steel sculptures. *Endless Column* is the artist's best-known work and marked a pivotal moment in his career. Commissioned for the "Sculpture and the Environment" exhibition in 1970, it was erected on the corner of Fifth Avenue and East Seventy-ninth Street in New York City, where it remained for about a year and a half. The artist intended his sculpture as a drawing in space that lifts the beholder's view upward in a staccato movement. The work represents an obvious homage to Brancusi's *Endless Column* (1937) and also refers to the Zen concept of a koan experience, in which an object becomes a means to an end, a "ladder in the sky." Streeter's interests continued to look skyward in his kite-making activities and constructions of tower-like structures. —UL

SELECTED REFERENCES: *Art that Flies* (Dayton, Ohio: Dayton Art Institute, 1991); *Tal Streeter: sky, moon, dragons, kites and smiles* (Verbank, New York, and Seoul, Korea: Romig House and Ahn Graphics, 1993).

Endless Column, 1968
Steel painted red
69'4" x 7'10" x 7'6"
Purchased with the aid of funds from the National Endowment of the Arts and gift of the Ralph E. Ogden Foundation, Inc.
1977.2

URSULA VON RYDINGSVARD

Born 1942 in Germany of Polish descent; lives in New York City. Von Rydingsvard was born in a German labor camp, and for five years following the end of World War II her family lived in a succession of eleven different camps for displaced persons. In 1950 she immigrated with her family to America. Von Rydingsvard artistically matured in the 1970s. She was influenced by the rigors of Minimalism but reacted against its cool aesthetics. Her oeuvre is connected both to geometric abstraction and to the organic, natural world. Von Rydingsvard's work reflects the brooding sensibility rooted in nature that characterizes Northern Romanticism. Her multivalent sculpture is imbued with a wide range of personal associations including many from her religious and family background (*For Paul* is dedicated to her husband), as well as the trauma of World War II. Monolithic and craggy, von Rydingsvard's site-specific *For Paul* measures up to the majestic topography of the surrounding Storm King and Schunnemunk Mountains.

Von Rydingsvard has taught at Pratt Institute, Fordham University, Yale University, and the School of Visual Arts, among other institutions. She holds an honorary doctorate degree from the Maryland Institute College of Art and has received grants from the New York State Council of the Arts (1978), the National Endowment of the Arts (1979, 1985, 1987), and the Creative Artists Program Service (1980). In 1983 she received a Guggenheim Fellowship. In 1996 von Rydingsvard was recipient of the Alfred Jurykowski Foundation Award in Fine Art. —UL

SELECTED REFERENCES: Dore Ashton, et al., *The Sculpture of Ursula von Rydingsvard* (New York: Hudson Hills Press, 1996); Michael Brenson and Deborah Emont Scott, *Ursula von Rydingsvard* (Kansas City, Missouri: Nelson-Atkins Museum of Art, 1997); Stephen Fleischman and Martin L. Friedman, *Ursula von Rydingsvard: sculpture* (Madison, Wisconsin: Madison Art Center, 1998); *Ursula von Rydingsvard, Sculpture* (Mountainville, New York: Storm King Art Center, 1992).

For Paul, 1990–92
Cedar and graphite
14'4" x 9' x 13'8"
Gift of Sherry and Joel Mallin, The Horace W. Goldsmith Foundation, Ann M. Hatch, Vera G. List, and Steven and Nancy Oliver
1994.1

Untitled, 1972
Aluminum and stainless steel
20' x 25'4" x 16'(overall)
Purchased with the aid of funds from the National Endowment for the Arts and gift of the Ralph E. Ogden Foundation, Inc.
1972.3.a–c

Two Circles, 1972
Aluminum and stainless steel
a. 18 x 24 x 18'
b. 18 x 24 x 18'
Gift of the Ralph E. Ogden Foundation, Inc.
1973.5.a–b

Untitled, 1969
Aluminum and stainless steel
10' x 16'x 9'½"
Gift of Mrs. Margaret H. Ogden
1979.6

DAVID VON SCHLEGELL

Born 1920, St. Louis, Missouri; died in 1992. The son of the American Impressionist painter William von Schlegell, he attended the Art Students League, where his father taught. He subsequently studied engineering and worked for Douglas Aircraft during the 1940s. Von Schlegell did not turn to sculpture until 1961, after he had spent more than a decade as a painter. During the 1960s and 1970s he worked mainly with industrial materials to create streamlined abstract works that reflected his knowledge of yacht and airplane design. Storm King features five of his abstract sculptures, including the first site-specific work commissioned by the Art Center: two vertical poles, each topped with a projecting archlike element. His best-known piece at Storm King is the series of three monumentally scaled, yet delicate cubic forms commissioned for the west field. From a side view, the thin metallic legs are barely perceptible, so that the white squares seem to hover in space, but seen from above, they appear to rest on the ground. Von Schlegell enjoyed critical success throughout his career. In 1971 he was appointed director of graduate studies in sculpture at the Yale School of Art, where he taught until his retirement in 1990.
—MB

SELECTED REFERENCES: *David von Schlegell* (Waltham, Massachusetts: Rose Art Museum, Brandeis University, 1968); *Immanence. Sculpture and Recent Painting of David von Schlegell* (New Haven, Connecticut: Yale University Art Gallery, 1993).

Untitled, 1969
Stainless steel and aluminum
39'6" x 27' x 8"
Gift of the Ralph E. Ogden Foundation, Inc.
1969.11.a–b

Untitled, 1969
Stainless steel
a. 8'‚ " x 9' 8" x 13‚ "
b. 64 x 52 x 81"
Gift of the Ralph E. Ogden Foundation, Inc.
1969.17.a–b

FRITZ WOTRUBA

Born 1907, Vienna, Austria, where he died in 1975. Wotruba is regarded as the father of Austrian post World War II sculpture. He sought to reinterpret the human figure by subjecting it to a more geometricized aesthetic. In its early phase, the ensuing abstraction, as illustrated in *Man Walking*, resulted in heavy, block-like forms of archaizing roughness, which still contained considerable anatomical details. A limestone version of this sculpture was chosen to represent Austria at the Venice Biennale in 1952. In the late 1950s, his figures became slender and columnar; in the sixties they were reduced to pillar-like constructions. Since his appointment to the Vienna Academy of Fine Arts, Wotruba has taught an entire new generation of sculptors, and has been actively involved in the cultural revival of Austria. —UL

SELECTED REFERENCES: Otto Breicha, *Wotruba und his Orbit— Schüler—Freunde—Zeitgenossen*, Galerie und Auktionshaus Hassfurther, Vienna, 1995; *Fritz Wotruba, Druckgraphik 1950–1975*, Graphische Sammlung Albertina, Vienna 1989.

Man Walking, 1952
Bronze
61½ x 17¼ x 24"
Gift of the Ralph E. Ogden Foundation, Inc.
1963.38

Design: Katy Homans

Editing and production supervision: Sally Fisher

Color separation, printing, and binding: Mondadori Printing S. p. A., Verona, Italy